Ghosts of the Southern Mountains and Appalachia

Ghosts of the Southern Mountains and Appalachia

Nancy Roberts

University of South Carolina Press

Copyright © University of South Carolina 1988

Published in Columbia, South Carolina, by the
University of South Carolina Press

Enlarged edition of Appalachian Ghosts published by Doubleday & Company, Inc.,
Garden City, New York, 1978

Photographs by Bruce Roberts

07 06 05   10 9 8 7

Library of Congress Cataloging-in-Publication Data

Roberts, Nancy, 1924–
    Ghosts of the southern mountains and Appalachia.

    Enl. ed. of : Appalachian ghosts. c1978.
    1. Ghosts—Appalachian Region. I. Roberts, Nancy,
1924–   Appalachian ghosts. II. Title.
BF1472.U6R63 1988   133.1'0975   88–20836
ISBN 0–87249–597–3
ISBN 0–87249–598–1 (pbk.)

CONTENTS

Ghosts of the Southern Mountains and Appalachia

Night of the Hunt

Hendersonville, North Carolina

In the North Carolina mountains south of Asheville and nearer Hendersonville, it was a good hunting night. You might even go so far as to say, it was the best of all nights and the worst of all nights for after it, neither dog nor hunters would ever be the same again. It is too bad, because this particular dog was his owner's pride and joy.

It was the time of year when it began to get dark early but wasn't too cold, and the sky was full of shifting clouds. Wheeler and his friend, Tom McDuffy, were riding along in Wheeler's old blue Ford pick-up along Highway 25 south of Hendersonville. String Bean, a black and tan coon dog, was in the back, and to hear Jim Wheeler tell it, no dog ever lived that was this one's equal. He began to explain to his inexperienced friend how the hunt goes.

"Coons like dark nights and they tree better on nights like this instead of just heading for a hole in the ground," explained Jim who had been trying to talk his friend into going with him for a long time.

"Tom, it gets into your blood and in the fall when the darkness begins to come early, you think about walking through the leaves, seeing your breath make smoke curls in the night air and watching the sky hoping the moon's not going to come out and light up the whole woods."

"What are we trying to do, though?"

"Well, the purpose of coon hunting is to tree the coon."

"Yes, I know that but to me String Bean's no different from other dogs, You act like he's human."

"What are you talking about. String Bean's won more coon hunt trophies than any dog in North or South Carolina either. I did hear onetime there was a dog over in Tennessee that had won just as many; but that may have been String Bean's grand-daddy. Tennessee's where all the great coon dogs come from, though."

"What makes one of these 'great coon dogs' you're talkin' about?"

"Well, I'll tell you. They got to be able to run all night and they got to have a nose that can tell the trail of a coon from a possum."

"What else?"

"Now, take String Bean, when he's after a coon nothing in heaven or earth's goin' to distract him. A deer could start 'buck dancing' right in front of him and he'd pass on by. But the main thing about a

good dog is his bark. As soon as String Bean picks up the scent he'll bark to let me know and then, as he chases the coon, he'll bark every couple of minutes to let me know which direction he's running in. That's his trailin' bark."

"What kind of bark does that one sound like?"

"Well, it's not his regular bark. You just get so you know it. Then when he's got the raccoon treed he'll give out a series of continuous barks. String Bean can just about talk to me," said Jim proudly.

By this time the two men had reached a side road north of Flat Rock where they turned off. They bounced down the rutted dirt road, skirting pot holes, for several miles on the way to their favorite hunting spot. The woods they were headed for was just the other side of the old Culpepper place not far from Pisgah Forest. When the pick-up rolled to a stop, Jim let String Bean out of the back of the truck and started talking to him.

"You're gonna have a good time tonight, String Bean. The weather's just right for us and that coon." Only the silhouettes of the bare tree branches could be seen against the dark sky. Gnarled limbs of oak trees gestured awkwardly overhead, a few beeches still wore some of their bright brown leaves and the big tulip poplars stood like white skeletons in the night. The hunters adjusted and lighted their carbide lamps fixing them to their caps. String Bean watched and waited. He knew the night was his and there would be coons out there just for him.

At last they were ready to take the dog off his leash. With a "Go get 'um!" from Jim, String Bean was off. For a few seconds his paws could be heard hitting the carpet of old leaves on the ground as he circled about in the woods, then the rustling sounds faded and the men were left in the darkness and quiet of the Carolina woods. They were far enough away from Hendersonville so that there was no reflection of lights in the sky nor a sound to be heard from the distant highway. It was like being the last two men alive.

The carbide lamps made them look almost like coal miners in some dark, deep tunnel rather than hunters. Actually, it was past the season when you could shoot raccoons and neither man carried a gun. They were there to hear the dog run, to get away from their wives for an evening and for something else they couldn't have put into words if they tried. Perhaps, it was to experience that awesome feeling of being remote from civilization, out there alone in the woods on this ink-black night.

Whatever each man's thoughts were, they were interrupted by a bark. String Bean's voice floated back saying he had found the trail of a coon. Jim and Tom stood leaning against the truck. Now they would wait until the dog's bark indicated he had the coon treed. When it came they would make their way to him while String Bean would give out almost continuous barks to keep the coon in the uppermost branches and the hunters on course to the tree.

Another trailing bark came a minute later from beyond the far side of the hill, and then another but Wheeler heard nothing that sounded like the bark of a dog who has the coon treed. After the two barks a long silence followed. "That's not like String Bean to go all this time without barking," said Jim after they had waited about ten minutes. Tom didn't reply but he felt a chill as if the night had suddenly turned cold, which it hadn't. They walked around the truck restlessly, the beams from the carbide lamps on their caps darting back and forth, as they turned their heads this way and that, hoping to hear something from out there in the darkness.

"You've 'muched' over that dog so, I'd like to know where he is now," said Tom. Jim didn't reply to the jibe. This hadn't happened before and he waited for his dog's voice to tell him which way to go.

Then it came but it was no trailing bark. He had never heard String Bean sound that way for this was a long, frightened, wailing bark as if the animal had run into something he could not ken, something far beyond the edge of his knowledge. Without saying a word the men started off through the darkness in the direction of the last unearthly yelp, their pale beams of light painting the tree branches white wherever they swept across them.

They got their bearings as they crested the hill. Ahead of them lay a little 'basement' of blackness where the ruins of the old Culpepper place stood, surrounded by a tangle of vines. Betwixt them and the house lay a pond and beyond it they now saw a dim pinpoint of light. They were making their way carefully around the pond toward the house and were just at the water's edge, when they heard it for the first time. It was a sound that floated and hung suspended in the darkness. Melodic, lingering it seemed to wrap each note around them leaving a plaintive trail in the air.

"Nobody's lived in that house in over fifty years," said Jim.

"Well, somebody is in there now," said Tom trying to tell himself that he wasn't really hearing anything out of the ordinary. For the first time since they had started out, they heard a whimper and it came from the direction of the house.

It was String Bean and he was on the front porch, his nose pointing to the door. Now and then, he would whimper again. The two men crept up closer, the candlelight from one of the windows their guide.

"Who could be living in this old wreck of a place?" Tom seemed to think he had to whisper.

"I don't rightly know."

"Well, I hope it ain't hants."

"I'm goin' to knock," said Jim and knock he did, but nobody opened the door. For a few seconds there was silence and then inside the house a fiddle struck up an old tune that was somewhere in Jim's memory but too far back for him to get a hold on.

"I hear music and dancing."

"Must be having a party in there and just can't hear us," said Tom.

He struck the door several hard licks with his fist. But the fiddling went on unabated and no one came to the door. Suddenly they heard thunder and a gust of wind fingered the sprigs of the shrubs against the house.

"Let's go. It's goin' to set to rainin'."

"No it's not. I want to see in the window," said Jim. They stopped in front of a high window with an old brick chimney beside it.

"Lift me up some, Tom. I got to see those people in there. Tom made a stirrup of his hands and the other man pulled himself up enough to look in. The scene before him would stay with Jim Wheeler the rest of his life. A cold chill went through him. As Wheeler watched he began to tremble.

"Jim. You're shakin' so I can't hardly hold you up. What's the matter?" Jim Wheeler didn't answer but just kept staring in the window. Tom had now managed to pull himself up enough to see in, too. Both men were transfixed by the macabre scene before them. A bride and groom were dancing together. When the set ended the girl, dressed in a yellowed wedding dress, started toward the table with the candle on it.

She's going to put it out thought Jim but as he watched her reach the table, he was dumbfounded to see her pass right through it! The train of her wedding dress brushed across the candle flame and it never even flickered! Wheeler's heart turned a cartwheel but he clung to the sill with one foot on the chimney and the other lodged in a place where a board was off. Then he saw them start up again swirling and tromping, looking at each other as though hypnotized and not getting a mite out of step as they moved rhythmically to the sound of fiddle and banjo.

How long the two hunters continued to watch, neither knew. Perhaps it was minutes or perhaps just seconds when suddenly the candle within was extinguished and all was dark and quiet. Both men dropped to the ground. Tom stepped on a brick, fell, picked himself up and then he and Jim were running a foot race to see which could leave the fastest. Fortunately, Wheeler thought to stop and call String Bean and the dog was soon beside them, glad to be in human company again. Branches slapped against their faces as they ran and the briars were like sharp claws tearing at their clothes some piercing the flesh beneath. It didn't matter. In their haste, they ran wide of the truck and had to stop and get their bearings before they finally found it.

Wheeler didn't take String Bean out again that winter and the next season he found another hunting place miles north of Hendersonville. But there was a hard to define difference in both man and dog. Jim noticed that it was a long time before his pleasure in the hunt returned. As for String Bean, it was months before his bark took on its old, confident tone and sometimes Wheeler thought it would never again sound the way it once had. The dog had felt whatever was happening there as surely as the men had seen it. It wasn't menacing, it just wasn't part of this world, something that animals are often aware of even before people.

The story of the dancing bride has been told by the old people of the area for many years and Jim and Tom were not the first to hear the music and see the ghostly pair celebrate their vows. Finally, a researcher discovered that in the late 1890s an elaborate wedding had taken place there but the bride, sticken with scarlet fever, had died a few weeks later.

Some say the spirits of the bride and groom are this young couple continuing to return almost a century later to celebrate their wedding day. Not

long ago a man near Flat Rock told the story of what
he had seen.

"The fiddler's were just fiddlin' away and when
a voice sang out 'Swing your partner,' you've never
seen a girl float through the air like that one did
when the groom swung out his bride. Even now, it
gives me cold chills all the way down my spine just to
think about it." The group listening to him were
silent.

Then, an eighteen year old boy spoke up, "I'm
ready to go out there tonight if somebody will go
with me." But no one volunteered or even looked
his way and the story teller went on talking medita-
tively.

"It was about five years ago late at night when I
passed that way. Some says in my grand-daddy's
day there used to be young 'uns all over the place,
foreigners comin' from way off and lots of play par-
ties. A fine house stood there 'oncet'. I'm a 'goin'
back some day 'cause I want to see that bride and
groom dancing together one more time before I
die, but not right yet."

Return of the Bell Witch

Adams, Tennessee

"I think she is back," says Carney Bell, descendant of the man whose death the Bell Witch is said to have caused. Mr. Bell, one of the owners of Austin and Bell Funeral Home at Springfield, Tennessee has had experiences that prove to him that the most famous witch of the nineteenth century is here and up to her old tricks.

"Not long before my mother died, she was frightened and called me to come over and check the house. She had heard a loud series of crashes and stayed in her bedroom calling me from the upstairs phone. Mother lived about five doors from our home. When I arrived I checked every door—there are seven outside doors—and every one of them was locked. But when we went in the pantry her best glassware had fallen from the shelves and lay all over the floor. The shelves ranged from four to six feet from the floor and yet nothing was broken! If I hadn't seen it for myself I wouldn't have believed it."

How could some malevolent being, who first appeared almost 200 years ago, still roam the area north of Nashville, near Adams, Tennessee today? Yet, that is exactly what seeems to be happening. The account of the Bell Witch is probably the most widely documented story of the supernatural in America, not only because of the marker erected to her by the State of Tennessee Department of Archives and History, but because so many people have had a personal encounter with her.

After causing John Bell's death she announced she would be gone for a century, but that has past. Now, people like W. M. Eden who owns a portion of the original Bell farm, John Bell's descendant, Carney Bell, and numerous others believe the Bell Witch has come back just as she promised to do.

Heaven knows that Kate had every reason to return in the first place. In the opinion of this writer, few apparitions come back to haunt any of us for revenge. They simply happen to be there—at the same place we are at the same moment in time. But that does not include this particular spirit who some say suffered at the hands of one man. She returned for revenge.

"I believe in Kate," says W. M. Eden. He is a white-haired man, dressed in a blue plaid shirt and overalls. "She's never hurt me but there have been nights when I have had to really fight just to keep the covers on my bed; and I've heard footsteps as near to me as that bedroom door." But let us go back many years and to another state where the story first began.

In the late 1770s a hard-working young man named John Bell lived alone in his cabin in Halifax County, North Carolina. He was not planning to remain alone, however, for he was engaged to a lady who owned a large tract of farm land. Her name was Kate Batts, a prominent name belonging to one of the first settlers of eastern North Carolina. After her husband's death, John Bell had stopped at her farmhouse now and then to help her with the settling of the estate. Less than a year after she had donned the black widow's attire, which only accentuated her white skin and cloud of waist length black hair, the pair announced their engagement.

But scarcely were they engaged when John began to learn that the widow had a vile temper and a sharp tongue. He searched for ways to break off with Kate but she would not listen. The farm was more than she could handle alone and she was determined that John Bell would become her husband and farm it. The unfortunate man, who had been blind enough to think this woman capable of any love or kindness, could only imagine what it would be like to live with her. He was in torment.

On a winter afternoon they had been out riding over Kate's farm and discovered that a building of hers needed repairing. John's tools were at his cabin and when they rode over there to get them, the widow was thirsty. As she drew water from the

3C 38

BELL WITCH

To the north was the farm of John Bell, an early, prominent settler from North Carolina. According to legend, his family was harried during the early 19th century by the famous Bell Witch. She kept the household in turmoil, assaulted Bell, and drove off Betsy Bell's suitor. Even Andrew Jackson who came to investigate, retreated to Nashville after his coach wheels stopped mysteriously. Many visitors to the house saw the furniture crash about them and heard her shriek, sing, and curse.

TENNESSEE HISTORICAL COMMISSION

This is the only historic sign known that commemorates a witch! Recent accounts indicate that the witch is back after her absence of a century.

well, a freak accident occurred and she was struck in the forehead by the heavy bucket. She gave a little cry and collapsed. John bathed her face but, unable to revive her, began to fear she was dead.

His next thought was that others would believe he was to blame. Carrying the limp form down to his root cellar beneath the house, he left her there. Unlike some cellars of this sort, it could be locked from within the house by means of a trap door.

That night and all the next day everything was quiet. Terrified over his predicament, he knew he must soon find a place to bury her. Then, as he prepared for bed, he heard a sound near his hearth and just above the root cellar. It was a dragging sound followed by moans. In the middle of the night he was still awake; and it must have been two in the morning when he heard his name called.

"John, help me. Please help me." He tried to believe he had heard nothing. But the sounds went on. "I'm so hungry. Water . . . please." And so it went for the rest of the night. His dog began sniffing the crack around the trap door and with a kick, John sent the dog hurtling out of the cabin. He examined all the possibilities. If he brought her up, she would cause a scandal because of his leaving her down there so long. The only way to keep her from doing that would be to go ahead and marry her and that was unthinkable. He knew she would never let him go, and her temper was such that she would have her own way or die in the attempt. Realizing this, he knew what he had to do. He did not open the trap door.

The next morning he was exhausted but he spent the day taking care of his animals and repairing some of his own farm buildings. By late afternoon when he returned the faint cries had ceased and all was quiet. When he cautiously entered the root cellar with a candle late that night, he found she was dead. Loading the body on the sled he used to haul firewood, he pulled it to her house and around back beside her own well. There he left it. An old half-blind crone who sometimes helped Widow Batts with the vegetable garden discovered Kate the next morning.

For several months it was as if a tremendous weight had been lifted from him. He met a kind, understanding young woman named Lucy Williams and soon proposed to her. John and Lucy Bell had not been married long when he decided to sell his farm in North Carolina and start a new life in Tennessee. Buying a thousand acre farm on the banks of the Red River about fifty miles north of Nashville not far from the Kentucky border, he brought his family to settle in Robertson County in 1804. But he was to have only a few peaceful years.

Walking along while plowing one day he looked over to see a monstrous, inky black bird with fiery eyes sitting on a fence post staring at him. He had never seen anything like it before. Even when he walked toward it the bird did not move but sat motionless, glaring fiercely at him. He shouted at it and the creature flew toward him swooping down as if to attack but swerving at the last second with a horrendous fluttering of wings. It passed above him so close that he was overwhelmed by the most dreadful stench as it barely cleared the top of his head. That was the first peculiar event he would later remember.

It is not easy to pin down when the scraping of pear tree branches against the large one and one-half story log house and other normal noises made a transition to sounds of the most eerie nature. According to one of his sons, Richard, he and his three brothers were asleep in an upstairs bedroom and awakened to hear a noise like an enormous rat gnawing on the bedpost. They got up to investigate but as soon as a candle was lit all was quiet and nothing could be seen. The moment the candle was blown out, the noise began again.

This horrible, gnawing sound was soon heard every night and it moved from one room to another in the Bell house. Then came a series of most repulsive noises as if someone were smacking their lips while they ate, alternating with loud gulps that resembled choking or strangling. And if it seemed that there was peace for a few hours, in the midst of the family's relieved slumbers the covers would be jerked off their beds as if snatched by some unseen hand. But worst of all, an invisible presence twisted and jerked the children's hair until they ran screaming in fright.

At first the Bell's said nothing to anyone about these events. Finally, John Bell told his close friend and neighbor Jim Johnson and the Johnsons came over to spend the night. It was to be the most unpleasant night of their lives.

They had no sooner retired than the noises started. It began with loud knocking followed by gnawing, scratching and smacking. The chairs in the Johnsons' bedroom overturned. Bedcovers flew off. The Bell's daughter, Betsy, was slapped across the face by invisible hands and the entire house was soon in pandemonium. The Johnsons could hardly be expected to keep all this to themselves and when word was out about the strange happenings the curious began to arrive from all over Tennessee.

Some came to investigate and others to help if they could. About this time another mystifying spectacle occurred. Lights could be seen flitting through the trees in the Bell yard and across the fields of the farm.

Now, the family began to try to talk to whatever it was by asking questions such as how many people are in the room, how many horses are in the yard or whatever could be answered with a number of knocks. The answers were always correct. And then the thing began to talk. Words first came in a harsh, disembodied voice that gradually gained strength and grew more feminine. It was soon apparent that the thing had a passionate hatred for John Bell and whether it first revealed its identity to him or some other member of the family, all soon knew it as, Kate Batts' witch.

When Bell first learned this he went into deep depression. Not that he was the only person who was the object of her attentions, but it was for him that she reserved her most vicious acts and now that she could be understood, her oath to kill him was unmistakable.

But for many it was a most entertaining phenomenon. The question often arose as to whether you can touch a ghost. Visitors to the Bell house were curous about this, and on one occasion Calvin Johnson, who Kate frequently talked with, asked her if he could shake her hand. She was reluctant to do this but finally agreed that she would do so if he

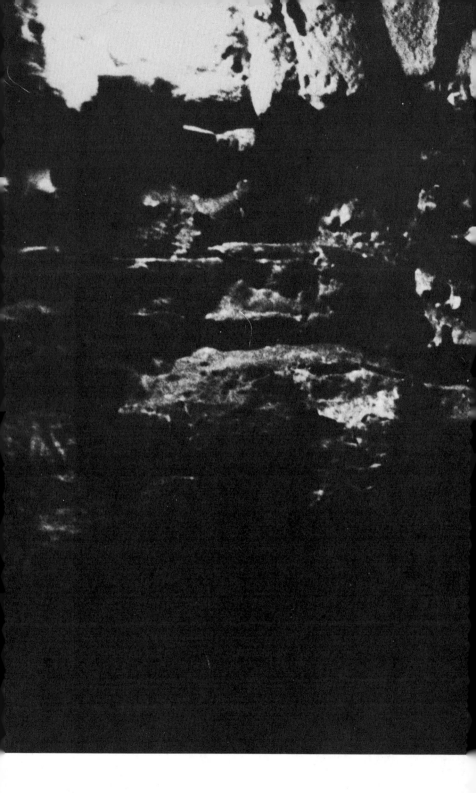

This cave where the witch is said to have made her home is on a portion of the old Bell farm north of Nashville.

would promise not to try to hold or grasp her hand. He stretched out his hand and within seconds something soft lay in it, like the hand of a woman. No one doubted him who was watching his expression when it happened. His brother, Jack, made the same request but Kate refused him saying, "No, I don't trust you. You are a grand rascal, Jack Johnson."

Visitors sometimes found Kate embarrassing as she revealed their darkest secrets, poked fun at them, joined blasphemously in religious discussions and when she raided a nearby still house she would keep everyone up all night with her frightful oaths and drunken singing. Kate performed for a constant stream of visitors and about this time an entire "family" of spirits joined her at the Bell farm. Now, there were five distinct disembodied voices including Kate's. While the other four spirits came and went, Kate stayed with the Bell family and, particularly, with John Bell; but she would never explain why she hated him so.

Two years went by and John Bell began to suffer mysterious attacks in which his tongue would swell and stiffen in his mouth. He would be unable to eat or talk and described the feeling as similar to having a sharp stick wedged crossways in his mouth. Kate would interrupt the concern of his wife and family when he was having these spells by laughing raucously at his suffering. His afflictions grew more frequent and more terrible almost making him an invalid and the witch cursed him viciously all the while.

On the morning of December 19, 1820 his wife was unable to wake him from an unnaturally deep sleep. His son, John, Jr., went to the medicine cupboard but his prescription bottle was missing and in its place was another vial with a dark, smoky liquid. As usual, Kate was among them.

"I've got him this time," she crowed gleefully. "He'll never get up from that bed again," said Kate. And she was right, he never did.

When asked about the vial in the cupboard she replied, "I put it there myself. I gave Old John a big dose of it last night while he was asleep and that fixed him." The family put some of the liquid on a straw and drew it through a cat's mouth sending the animal into an immediate convulsion. John Bell died the next day. Even at his funeral Kate disrupted the solemn ceremony with raucous, drunken singing during the burial service in the family graveyard.

In 1821, the witch surprised everyone by announcing that she was leaving but would return in seven years. Her homecoming in February of 1828 was marked by a return of the knockings, gnawings, and scratchings on the outside walls of the house and the pulling off of covers from the beds. This time, however, the Bell Witch stay was brief. After Mrs. Bell's death the farm was divided, and it was not surprising that no one wanted to live in the old house which was eventually torn down. But this was not to be the end of the Bell Witch. As she left, she swore to return in a hundred years. Recent events indicate her promise is being fulfilled.

In a publication called the "Tennessee Traveler," Don Wick writes of encounters people are having with the Bell Witch in the twentieth century in the cave near the banks of the Red River. They report various phenomena such as the figure of a dark-haired woman floating through the cave passages, the sounds of chains dragging along the stone floor, footsteps and unearthly cries. W. M. Eden who has owned this part of the Bell farm for many years has had his share of personal experiences "with Kate or whatever it is inside that cave."

"On a winter's day a few years ago there was new snow on the ground. I heard someone knocking at my front door and looked through the window. When I saw the outline of a figure I didn't recognize I went to get my shotgun. By the time I returned, the form was walking toward a large tree in the yard but it never came out on the other side, so I went out the back door and around to the tree but found no one. My shoes were making prints in the fresh snow but from the front door to the tree the snow was as smooth and undisturbed as if it had just fallen and there were no footprints at all."

Carney Bell, one of the present day descendants of John and Lucy Bell, has had his own odd experiences in recent years which he attributes to Kate.

"Some things that have happened in the family are almost like a coincidence. For instance when I was watching television one night and a next door neighbor called to tell me there was a program on one of the channels about the Bell Witch, I turned to that channel but could only get wavy lines. After trying two other sets in the house, we gave up. Yet I found that the neighbors on each side of us were viewing it!"

According to Eden, a group of soldiers from Fort Knox, Kentucky came to explore the dark, dank recesses of the cave and one of the soldiers poked fun at the story of Kate. "A few minutes later he was lying on the floor of the cave. He shouted for help saying he could feel something sitting on his chest and squeezing the breath right out of him. I don't think he will forget his sensation in that cave when something grasped him and pinned him to the ground."

Strange, floating lights appear in the fields of the farm owned by W. M. Eden, and many have chased the elusive lights only to have them vanish and reappear a short distance away. In this area around Adams, Tennessee, the Bell Witch is not just a legend—she is a strong presence.

My own visit to the cave was an interesting, if eerie, experience. As we came out into the welcome, fresh night air, Mr. Eden stopped and looked back over his shoulder. There was an air of expectancy about the way he stood there looking back at the cave as if he might see something emerge at any moment.

That night there was no sign of anything in the darkness behind us, but Eden told of the time "I was in the cave with my German shepherd dog, Fritz, when we heard a sound back in the innermost recesses of the cavern as if a heavy object was being dragged noisily along the stone floor. I sat down on a ledge to see what would happen and Fritz sat quietly beside me. The sound grew closer and louder. I knew something was about to round the curve in the wall of the cavern just a few feet away.

"At that point Fritz who weighs at least 75 pounds leaped into my lap! The noise grew louder and whatever it was went right past us while the dog huddled against me and I could feel the animal trembling. After waiting for two or three minutes, we both raced for the entrance. What was it? I think it was Kate." Eden believes that her spirit roams the Adams area day and night.

"I've known for years that cave is a strange place; but it's where Kate lives now. They say she was gone for a hundred years but, I believe she's home for good."

When this story was written the cave could be toured by contacting Mr. W. M. Eden of Adams, Tennessee.

The Shenandoah Stage

New Market, Virginia

Two young Confederate officers sat eating together in the dining room of the Hotel in New Market, Virginia on the evening of May 24, 1862. General Stonewall Jackson, who would become Lee's right arm, had just won his first important battle the day before at Front Royal. Was there any way for the Union to stop him now? Perhaps, and perhaps not.

The officers had seen the man seated at the bar looking at them and decided he must be a Confederate sympathizer. Judging by his lack of a pistol, his imported suit and well manicured hands he could be a writer or a minister visiting in the New Market area, perhaps, en route to Richmond. Fleming raised a gray clad arm gesturing for him to join them and the stranger responded eagerly.

Slim and immaculately groomed, the dark-haired young man sat down introducing himself as John Sharp, and as he spoke there were traces of a British accent. After a few minutes of evaluating him, both officers had decided that he was British and sympathetic to the Southern cause. Lt. Henry Fleming voiced his gratitude for the Enfield rifles that had been getting through the blockade and the gentleman smiled and nodded.

"Why is England so slow to recognize the Confederacy formally?"

"Mr. Fleming, I don't know, but I understand it will not be long before an ambassador will be sent to Richmond."

"Of course England needs our cotton if the textile mills are to keep running," said Lt. MacRae. "Isn't that so?"

"My dear friend, I can assure you that even now, important decisions are being made in England."

"Important decisions have been made here and it's time they did something to recognize us," said Stewart MacRae who was a South Carolinian.

"Columbia is such a beautiful city. I greatly enjoyed my recent stay there," said John Sharp changing the subject. His accent was pleasant to the ears of MacRae whose hopes for an education abroad had been postponed because of the war.

"You have just come from Columbia then?"

"Indeed I have. Is it possible I met your sister at a musical there . . . no, surely not. That would be too much of a coincidence. I think this girl's name was . . ."

"Letitia?"

"Of course. I recall it because this Letitia exemplified everything I had imagined about Southern womanhood."

"I can't believe it. You met my dearest sister. And how was she?"

"She was delightful."

"I don't know when I have had a letter from her but the mail doesn't keep up with General Jackson, you know."

"They say his men worship him now."

"He takes care of them—with General Banks' storehouses of supplies! Jackson manages to see that we get more than our fair share," said Fleming with a smile. Everyone joked about the way Jackson kept capturing the Union General's supplies and they even called Banks, "Jackson's commissary."

"You gentlemen will be resting here in New Market for a week or so, now, won't you?" said Sharp.

Fleming stiffened ever so slightly and the glass of wine on the way to his lips stopped in midair. "Why do you ask, sir?"

"Just an off-hand remark. I imagine the men jolly well need it for they have been on the march a great deal and I would think they must be tired. What do you say, MacRae?"

"Well, sometimes the men say he is 'marching them to death to no good end' but I know the General when he gets started. Winchester is only a few miles up the . . ."

"Hush! Stewart. We don't know what the General's got in his mind. No one does," said Lt. Fleming.

At that moment a courier approached the two Confederate officers and told them they were to join their regiment at once.

"We're marching?" asked MacRae and the courier nodded.

"Where is the good fellow who sat with you gentlemen?" asked one of the bartenders as they paid their bill.

"The Britisher?"

"He isn't a Britisher, he went to Harvard."

"Harvard?"

"Yes. My brother went there and picked up the accent. I knew I'd heard it before and I asked him. He finally admitted it, but said he had always been a Southern sympathizer." Fleming shook his head and grasped MacRae by the arm. "Did you hear that?"

"Certainly. But I know a Southern sympathizer when I meet one." They passed Sharp who was part of a group outside the hotel without noticing him.

The valley stage had just pulled up. The passengers and driver were entering the hotel for the evening meal. The stage was a familiar sight on the road to Winchester thought Sharp; and then an idea came to him as he stood there alone for a moment in the dusk. The thought was at once so practical and opportune that he leaped up into the driver's seat and seized the reins. In the interval since the vehicle had arrived, the street in front of the New Market Hotel had emptied and it seemed there was no one to see his deed. The stage was off to a mud-splattering, clattering start.

When he reached the edge of town, Sharp cracked his whip to urge the horses on. And, so, with this stage rode the fate of General Banks at Winchester and Stonewall Jackson's army on the way to attack.

Back in New Market the two young Confederate officers were saddling their horses in the stable next to the hotel building. There was no reason to hurry because it takes an army of 17,000 men more than a few minutes to get started. They had heard the clatter of the stage as it left and now looked up amazed to see the driver come running into the stable shouting, "Help! Someone has stolen my stage."

They cantered around to the front of the hotel and Fleming saw the man he had talked to at the bar. "Where is our Harvard man?" he called out and the fellow shook his head and replied, "He rushed off without paying his bill!"

"Let's go, Stewart. Spur your horse!"

"What do you mean? We've got a long road ahead of us."

"Our friend in the Hotel has taken off in the valley stage. He was a spy and we gave away Jackson's plan."

"Good Lord! We've got to stop him before he reaches the Union lines and warns Banks," said MacRae. And so, the "great valley chase" started there in the last twilight of May 24th, 1862. Ahead, the stagecoach pulled by four slightly worn horses followed by two young Confederates on fresh mounts. The stage probably had a two mile lead as they left New Market but the officers were Jackson's men and they were more than good "foot cavalry" as they sometimes derisively called themselves, they rode well, too.

By the time they passed the crossroads at Mt. Jackson the lead had narrowed to a half mile. The stagecoach horses were tiring, not used to such a

wild pace. At Edinburg at midnight the Confederate officers could see the stage in the moonlight
only a few hundred yards in front of them. And at
the same time they saw the stage, Sharp saw his two
pursuers. They would catch him before he could
reach help—unless he used his Navy revolver. He
hated to do that. Odd, that it had been MacRae's sister he met, and for one of the few times in his life,
he was much taken with a woman. What irony to
have to shoot the girl's brother. He cursed to himself. He wished now he had never followed his intu-
ition and asked MacRae her name back at the Hotel.

The smell of rain had been in the air earlier at
Mt. Jackson and now it had started. Cool drops
tapped his face as the stage swept under the storm.
What a spectacle the lightning was! He might not
have tó do anything, he thought. Most horsemen
were afraid of lightning and rightfully so. Of
course, it could strike the stage but caught up in the
excitement of the chase he laughed aloud for he
loved danger. Anyway, would the Devil harm his
own? Or, if God was really on the Union side, he
was safe either way!

But his pursuers, now only a short distance
behind him, were undiscouraged by the sharp
cracks of lightning so Sharp turned on the seat and
took aim. He knew what he had to do and he would
not miss. He could see the dark shapes of the two
horsemen and he did not know which was MacRae
and which was Fleming in the blackness. And then
he had a moment of indecision. He had shared a
meal with these two men and liked them both so
they were no longer strangers. But what was his

alternative? If he stopped he would become their prisoner and very likely be hanged. He would not, could not do that. Sharp had learned marksmanship well and he waited for them to ride even closer before he sighted down the barrel. Then he pulled the trigger.

As he did so a blast engulfed the stage but it came not from the pistol but from the clouds. Lightning struck right on the metal barrel just as the pistol was about to fire engulfing the man and the stage; and thunder came at the same second as it often does when lightning hits close by. The two Confederates reined their horses to a stop, momentarily blinded by the flash; then came thunder crashing around them and rumbling off to the South. Neither man was sure what had happened until they saw the charred outlines of the stage.

They were alone in the darkness with a dead spy who had tried to kill them, their nostrils inhaling the strong smell of horses wet from a mixture of sweat and spring rain, the storm subsiding and Jackson's suprise attack building up somewhere out in the night. They rejoined their regiment and for many reasons the entire episode was one they never really cared to talk about.

On the next day General Stonewall Jackson attacked the Federal line at Winchester and broke it and General Banks' men fled desperately toward the Potomac. His army escaped destruction but it was a panic-stricken retreat, little better than a rout. The people of Winchester looked upon the Confederate troops as saviors giving them an ecstatic welcome almost "demented with joy."

Now Jackson's men knew what they had been marching for and bitterness was replaced by elation over their dazzling triumph. Confidence in him and themselves soared and word of Jackson's feat spread as General Banks' star plummeted. The man who had stolen the stage, John Sharp, was no Britisher but, in reality a second lieutenant in the Union cavalry and the son of a wealthy Boston ship owner. His schooling had been at Harvard and his accent was deceptive. At Banks' request Lt. Sharp had volunteered to spy for the Union and was traveling up and down the valley collecting information on the movements of Stonewall Jackson's men.

A year later, Leland Hawes, a scout for Colonel Moseby, saw what he thought was the old valley stagecoach flying along at top speed, the horse's hoofs scarcely touching the ground. Its driver was glancing behind him as he urged his horses on. Then thunder rolled across the valley and clouds obscured the face of the moon. When they vanished, Hawes looked again but this time he saw nothing and for many years the stage was reported here and there between New Market and Winchester.

Only when the moon is full, only when rain is in the air and only when clouds drift over the face of the moon causing dark shadows is the stage seen again in our day. As it travels along old Highway 11, once called the Valley Pike, its fading red paint is splattered with mud and the driver's face is deadly pale and streaked by smoke. His bony, blackened hands grip the reins tightly as the stagecoach bounces over the ruts and stones of the old road.

But it's those four white horses that take your breath away to watch. In full gallop they strain at the creaking leather harness, manes flowing, hoofs flying. Why the hurry? Where are they going?

The stage is headed to Winchester more than a hundred years late, both driver and team captives of another dimension in time. They are destined to ride forever but never to arrive. How many visions like Sharp and the valley stagecoach are out there for us to encounter one of these nights on some remote mountain road or lonely deserted place? Like debris from this world left in space that will go whirling about forever, are we experiencing something left long ago on our planet from other lives, the eerie debris of the spirit-world?

Chain Gang Man

Decatur, Alabama

It was Sunday morning and he had been sitting
on the porch of his Pa's cabin back up in the Alabama hill country strumming his guitar and singing
to himself.

> "O hand me down that corpse of clay
> That I may look upon it.
> I might have saved that life,
> If I had done my duty."

The tune was, "Barbara Allen," and a sad one, but
for some reason the twenty-year old boy with curly
black hair and gentian blue eyes had always liked it.
To his surprise he saw a cloud of dust with a black
Ford in the midst of it come jouncing along the seldom traveled dead-end road. Two law men got out
of the car.

"You Lonnie Stephens?"

"Yeah, I'm Lonnie."

"Then come with us, an' if you come peacable, you won't get hurt."

Lonnie stood up in surprise and they took it for assent, but when they tried to put handcuffs on him he fought hard. It was not until they subdued him that he found out why they were here.

"We know you done killed her and you mought as well make a clean breast 'a it."

"Killed who?"

"Cordelia. Ain't that your girlfriend?"

"Dead? She can't be!"

"It was your gun what shot her. We done identified that and it wan't no trouble 'cause you dropped it in the woods right near her body."

Lonnie lifted both arms to bring the handcuffs down on the head of one of his captors but the other lawman saw his intention and butted him in the side so that he lost his balance and fell to the ground. "He resisted arrest all right," the man who had very nearly worn handcuffs on his head later testified at the trial. "He was like a wounded bobcat struggling to get shed of a trap! Scared me, he did."

Lonnie was brokenhearted over the murder of his sweetheart, but the law would not believe him. He hadn't killed her, he loved her and they were planning to get hitched come summer. How could the law convict him for something he hadn't done? But it was his gun and his girl and that was enough for the sheriff. When the judge delivered the sentence it was fifteen years on the chain gang. Lonnie was enraged for he knew that the real murderer was out there free as a mountain rattler while the best part of his own life would be gone. Sticks and stones can break your bones but words, he thought, yes, words *can* hurt you just the way you'd take a sharp knife to core an apple and throw the core on the ground to rot. That's what had happened to his life.

It was almost a matter of hours from that courtroom to the chain gang.

He could scarcely get out of the big metal cage at the prison camp because of the chain and the steel cuffs around each ankle; and he almost pitched forward on his face when he took his first step. His smile made you feel like smiling back. His eyes crinkled up at the corners when he was amused and his parents never had a lick of trouble with him. If anything he was almost too softhearted and would expend hours trying to nurse an animal back to health when it might just turn out to be a sickly critter at best. Lonnie Stephens didn't act like a killer.

It was his first day on the Alabama chain gang. Gripping the calves of his legs were leather straps meant to hold the steel cuffs up but they still scraped his ankles. The chain between the cuffs was shorter than a man's steps and was designed to keep him from running, but for Lonnie who was a tall fellow with a long stride, every step he took was like being in a sack race with a midget. Alabama had lots of rocks and all he could think about was that he had lots of time ahead of him.

When the man in the next cage passed the chain to him the first night to put through his cuff and hand to the next man he whispered as he turned to him, "Settle down mountain boy. This is a 'hard rock camp' and you just goin' to make it tough for yo'sef." He couldn't sleep well at first because each time a man moved during the night the chain tugged everybody else on the line. But he got used to it and to getting up with the men before daylight.

He tried to join the others as they sung—"Wa-a-ater boy. Where are a you hidin'. If you don' 'a come, gonna fetch yo', mammy." And then the faster chorus. "Gonna hit that rock, boys, from here to Macon, from heah to Macon. . . . " At first he didn't join in but soon he knew why the caged men sang. While they were working on the roads, singing was the only thing that seemed to ease the feeling of hurt inside.

In the middle of the day the guards handed out cans of beans and the water boy came around with a dipper. The sun moved higher and higher overhead as he broke rock with the sledge hammer and rolled it to the pile with his bare hands. His shirt was drenched in perspiration and began to stick to his skin. Late that afternoon he left his sledge hammer where he was breaking rock and went over for a drink of cool water.

"Hey! You biggety mountain boy. Don' you know to ask for water? See that stake? Get over there!" His hands were tied high near the top of the stake and he saw one of the sunburned, stubble-faced guards standing spread-legged in front of him with a wide leather belt that had holes in it. "Take that shirt off'n him," ordered the guard. Sometime during the whipping Lonnie fainted. When he came to, the water boy was throwing water

on his face and his back hurt like nothing he'd ever felt before.

He moaned throughout the night. As soon as his back got well enough and he could think about something besides the pain he made up his mind he was going to either escape or be killed trying. While they were working on the road they could look down in the valley and along the sides of the mountain and see the cabins with their blue chimney smoke drifting up. His friend, Vester, said "Them ain't like other folks. They'll look out after us an' holp us ef we can git there."

A week later Lonnie was in his cage trying to read the only thing he had been able to bring with him. It was a small Bible Cordelia had given to him after he had declared his intention to marry her. A guard named Guthrie entered his cage and he looked up in surprise. "Take your dirty hands off'n the Bible. You ain't fit to touch it, you murderin' bastard," said he and he kicked it out of Lonnie's hands. Lonnie didn't say anything out loud but his mouth moved as he cursed Guthrie wordlessly and he reached to pick it up.

Guthrie promptly sent him to the "hole." Some of the prisoners called it the "box" because it was the severest form of punishment reserved for those who defied a guard. The box had a hard, rough, wooden floor and was fitted inside with chains. It was less than five feet by five feet—too short to stand in and not long enough to lie down in. Twice a day they brought Lonnie a slice of bread and a cup of water. The only thing he knew he could do to keep from going crazy in the horrible discomfort and darkness was to put his mind on something else. Lonnie thought about Branch Corey. He knew Corey had taken a fancy to Cordelia and that the man was infuriated because she had rejected him.

Lonnie was sure that Corey had killed Cordelia and set it up so Lonnie would be blamed.

Lonnie thought about somehow tollin' him down to the creek where Corey had kilt Cordelia and then chokin' him real slow. Didn't make no difference if they hanged him for it. It would be better 'n spending the time on the chain gang. Then he began to think more calmly about how he could establish his own innocence and get evidence that would convict Branch Corey.

After that first day in the hole, he calmed down some and knew he could never kill anybody. But if his lawyer and members of his family hadn't found any clues to convict Corey, he would bring him to justice himself. He knew during his trial that the murder weapon had his initials on it and did look like one of his guns. Branch Corey had admired a gun of his the fall before and asked if he could shoot it sometime. He had offered it to him then. Had he gotten someone to copy the gun and scratched the initials on it himself? If he had only told his lawyer about this during the trial. It was dumb not to think of it for it had happened almost a year ago, about the time he began seeing Cordelia. Ah. That was it! Even then Corey probably began to think about what he would do to get revenge.

He realized now that this confinement with no distractions was ideal for another purpose. He would spend it on something else just as important—figuring out the details of his escape. He could fade back into the mountains and never be caught by the law. Mountain folk were clannish and even if the law suspected he was up there somewhere, they might decide it wasn't worth the risk to come and get him. One of his own family might be able to track down who made the copy of his gun and indict Corey, powerful as he was in the area.

Gradually his escape plan took shape. Vester and another friend named Thurmond could help. They would be working on that mountain road and one day they would reach the right curve. The right curve would be where the front guard leading the line of fifty or sixty prisoners couldn't see far behind him. He could see the whole thing in his mind, the guard foreman walking in the middle alongside the men who would be spread out as they went around the curve.

On the hard wooden floor in the pitch black darkness of the hole the days crawled past but by the morning of the seventh day when he was to get out, he had planned everything down to the last detail. They would overpower the guard foreman, take his pistol and then keep him in front of the men. The guard in front wouldn't be able to shoot for fear of hitting the foreman. They'd shoot the guard in front in the legs if he didn't throw them his gun right off; and then they'd be gone. It had to happen fast for guards working men "under the gun" never aimed a warning shot, they always shot to kill.

An opportunity came less than a week after Lonnie was out of the hole and back on the chain gang again. The men were out working on Alabama Highway 11. It was late afternoon and Lonnie looked down to see blood on his shoe. The leg irons had begun to cut into the flesh on one ankle but he disregarded it. Each day Lonnie and Vester had managed to station themselves about mid-way along the column. Today, the lead guard happened to be Guthrie whom Lonnie hated and, as usual, the foreman was patrolling about halfway up the line of men

The front third of the strung-out prisoners had rounded the curve when Lonnie gave the signal. Vester who was a big, strong man in his early thirties jumped the foreman. But the blow to the guard's head did not prevent him from letting out one terrified yell for help.

It was heard by Guthrie but it alerted the prisoners, too, and since they knew the plan they had the advantage and were able to fall back quickly before the startled Guthrie realized what was happening. When he did, he was looking squarely into the foreman's gun aimed at him by Lonnie.

"I ain't shot squirrel and deer all my life for nothin' Guthrie," he called out. "Throw me your gun."

Guthrie hesitated, then threw it short of Lonnie and to one side. When Lonnie went for it, Guthrie charged him. There was the sound of a shot and the guard fell back dead. They took his keys. With a desperate, hobbling gait the men reached the prison bus. The old bus sped down the mountain road with Vester at the wheel driving as fast as he used to when he was running liquor. In about fifty miles they were almost out of gas and there was nothing to do but abandon the bus in the woods. Several of the men had files and one of Guthrie's keys had worked on most of the leg chains except for

Vester's. They needed to fan out to cabins in the area and find a change of clothes. In the truck tool box, Lonnie discovered a file and began using it quickly to free his friend.

Through the trees they could see the highway they had just left and as Lonnie filed hurriedly, they saw the prison camp truck pass. There go the "dog boys" said Vester. These were the prisoners the men reserved their deepest contempt for, the ones who helped the guards run down escapees.

"We better light out and go different ways, Vester. How much time we've got depends on how far down the road they let 'em out. Them dogs are gonna be confused for awhile by all the trails but then they'll settle down."

"You still got your prison suit on, Lonnie."

"Somebody will help me. I may even get a lift," and with his long legs at last free of the cruel shackles, Lonnie ran off alone through the woods in the gathering darkness.

Bob and Sandy Burns were married in her church in Decatur just as she had always wanted, despite the depression and hard times. It was September of 1935 and she and her husband of several hours were driving up Highway 11 in a borrowed Model A for a brief honeymoon at the Reed House in Chattanooga. The wedding had been at five, the reception at six, and now it was past eight as the car's headlights pierced the darkness north of Fort Payne. For late September, the evening was warm and Bob opened the front window.

On the old Model A Fords, the windshield could be opened and pushed forward on a hinge so that a space of several inches at the bottom sucked in the oncoming air and circulated it over driver and passenger. Sandy held her head back enjoying the cool night air flowing across her face. Bob pushed the gas pedal down more, for there were no other cars on the road tonight and he would be glad to arrive at the Reed House where he had made their reservation. They would finally be away from all the festivities, which both agreed had continued for almost too long.

Bob pressed the accelerator and the car gained speed. A mist was rolling in across the highway to give the landscape an almost otherworldly look for even the most familiar objects can be eerie at night when the ground fog rises. Sandy put her head on his shoulder and gave a little sigh of pleasure, for the stress of wedding preparations was over and she was thinking that the rest of the night belonged to them. But her pleasure was short lived. As the Model A's headlights swung around the curve, they both saw it at the same time.

As his foot hit the brakes Bob knew he had been going too fast and he also knew that if the figure didn't move out of the road he would hit it. There stood someone full in the path of his car reaching with arms outstretched toward them. As they approached they could see the tall figure of a man dressed in the black and white stripes of prison garb, his clothes tattered as if torn from running through heavy brush. But it was the face they were both riveted to for the expression did not look like that of a criminal. It was young with an imploring look and the way the mouth moved, Sandy was sure she could understand the words—"Help me!"

Time seemed to go into slow motion and every second was endless. The brakes were slowing the car but they were not slowing it fast enough and as the distance narrowed to a few feet, then inches— the figure just stood there making no effort to move. Bob braced himself for the impact and Sandy closed her eyes.

The car's bumper hit the figure but there was not the slightest jolt. Instead a huge, dark shadow rose up from the pavement and like the flow of air over the front hood, literally glided up the windshield. Sandy felt the wind flowing under the open glass turn icy cold and for a second it was as if part of the misty figure was being sucked in with the air! For an instant she felt faint. Astounded, Bob looked in the rear view mirror to see the man now standing behind the car still holding out his arm in the same beseeching appeal for help.

He slowed the Ford and pulled off the road to a stop and got out. There were no other cars in sight and he could just make out the figure in the red glow from the tail light. Then, in the distance, Bob heard the barking chorus of hound dogs as if on a chase and he turned his head in the direction of the sound. When he looked back there was no one to be seen. Sandy was at his side. The pair stood there in the damp, cool air with the barks of the dogs floating on it from afar. Then the yelps faded and an almost palpable quiet enveloped them.

There was nothing to do but to return to the car and continue their trip. The lights of the city would be a welcome sight, thought Sandy. Perhaps the excitement of the wedding had been too much. And then she spoke for the first time.

"Why did we stop, Bob?" He gave her an incredulous look.

"You know perfectly well why we stopped. We stopped because of the man there in the road. Didn't you see him?"

"Yes. I saw him but it was so strange I was beginning to doubt my senses."

"You thought we were both over tired but I'm not so tired that I've begun seeing men in striped prison clothes in the road."

"I know. I saw what he had on, too."

The next morning the Reed House delivered a bountiful Sunday breakfast to their room and a copy of the morning paper. Sandy was munching on a blueberry muffin as she read the headlines.

Then she saw the story. "Was This Man Innocent?" the bold headline asked, and beneath it she read, "Killed on Highway 11 in Alabama while attempting to escape; authorities now think Lonnie Stephens may have been innocent. It happened just a year ago last night. . . ." Sandy put down the paper. She recalled the imploring look on the face they had seen and now she knew what it meant.

Nor was this the only time people have seen the apparition of Lonnie Stephens on Highway 11, the mountain boy whose vindication finally came, but too late to save his life.

Fort Mountain

Fort Mountain, Georgia

Frank Willard decided that if he continued to go over in his mind the reasons the stock market had fallen, he still wouldn't know any more than any other broker. He just wanted to get away from Atlanta, to go where it would be peaceful and beautiful and that meant the mountains of North Georgia. He and Meg and their seven-year old daughter Sarah would stay in a cabin tonight rather than outdoors; because it was Friday and it took time to set up camp. But tomorrow night they would sleep under the stars on Fort Mountain.

"Dad, why are you taking that equipment? I've never even seen you use it before?"

"You haven't, punkin, but I think it may come in handy." He was constantly surprised by how observant Sarah was.

He had found some gear that he had used during his college years and he wanted to recapture the freedom from worry he had known more than a decade ago before the world grew so complicated. Not only had he lost much of his client's money but some of his own as well, for he believed in what he recommended and usually bought the same stocks for himself. North Georgia was one of his favorite places and he was looking forward to getting there, although the place they were staying tonight was a small cabin over a century old and very primitive. It was near Chadsworth. "Use it whenever you and your family want to get away," a friend had generously told him.

He was lucky that Meg and young Sarah were both good campers and seemed to enjoy it as much as he did. They reached the cabin about nine o'clock that night and were ready for bed. When they went in, he led the way with his flashlight and then it went out. "Don't worry, Dad, I've got mine," said Sarah and she handed it to him so Meg could light a candle. In a little while they had two kerosene lamps burning and Frank could see the log walls and an old fireplace with smoky stones across the top. What a musty odor the place had he thought and he doubted anyone had lived there in years.

There was no running water, just a pump on the back porch and he really didn't want to chance drinking from it. They washed their faces out at the pump and he and Sarah refreshed themselves with spring water from one of the jugs.

They were in bed in less than thirty minutes, when he was awakened by Sarah's voice coming from off in the distance saying, "Daddy, I can't sleep."

"You'll be asleep in a few minutes, honey," he replied.

A minute or so passed and he had just dozed off when the child's voice spoke up again. "Daddy, it's hard to sleep with all that music going on."

"Music? I don't hear a thing. Meg, do you hear any music?"

"No, I don't. What does it sound like, honey?"

"Well, it's banjoes and fiddles playing and it's out there in the front room."

"Sarah, you're just imagining that."

"No, Daddy. I've heard some of those songs at school but these are prettier."

"Well, you'll just have to enjoy them alone then because Dad and Mom are tired and we're going to sleep."

Next morning everyone slept late because the large trees shaded the cabin from the morning sunlight. They didn't try to cook but ate breakfast at a fast food place in Chadsworth.

"Daddy, when people die can they come back and play the music they used to play?"

"No. When they die they don't come back and play any music."

"Then where did the music come from that I listened to last night?"

"Sarah, I don't want to hear any more about that music. Sometimes you take teasing too far."

"All right, Dad, but. . . ." Her mother frowned at her and Sarah stopped. She looked out the window then and was very quiet.

As they drove up the mountain they could see the tall tulip poplars with their golden leaves fluttering in the breeze, gray trunks straight and tall and the woods on each side of the road were an artist's palette of colors. In the lemon light of Indian summer the dogwoods shook what crimson leaves they had left in a last act of defiance. A squirrel holding a hickory nut stood motionless staring out at the road from the edge of the woods. This was when the seasons turned and as they did there was always this pause, this magical suspension of time that made Frank feel that he and everything around him would go on forever, just as it was at that moment.

"Dad, is it all right if I don't go with you or mother?"

"Why is that?"

"I thought I'd go looking for those little things called British Soldiers that grow on logs or maybe mushrooms."

"That's fine but just don't eat any and don't get lost."

"Dad, when have I gotten lost?" Sarah looked indignant.

"You haven't. But take your compass anyway." And it was true, she had a good sense of direction and after the first few trips they hadn't worried about her at all. She was a pretty remarkable little girl, he thought proudly.

As a boy in his teens Frank loved to come here. It was his special place to get away from parents and other perplexities. Like everyone who sees the wall of stones at the foot of the mountain, he often wondered about the people who built it, "moon-eyed people with blond hair" the Cherokee legends called them. Long before Columbus was born a band of people of Welsh heritage had landed in Mobile Bay and somehow made their way to North Georgia.

The Cherokees had called them the "moon-eyed people" because it was believed that they worshiped the moon. They were also credited with seeing better at night than animals.

The last gold shreds of the dress a tulip poplar had worn since spring drifted down coming to rest on the wall where Frank sat and for the first time he thought about the size of the stones and their weight. Many of them were far heavier than he could pick up alone; and several people would be needed to move them. He visualized the hands that had lifted these stones and wondered about the people who had placed them here so long ago.

Actually a barrier of loosely piled stones, the wall extended almost a thousand feet around one side of the mountain from east to west. It was three to seven feet high and at intervals along it were round, shallow pits encircled by rocks that may have been used as sentry posts or watch fire pits. The legend of the Welsh who came over to this continent in 1170 under the leadership of Prince Modoc had much credibility. They must have thought the Alabama area would be more desirable than Wales, for according to the story part of their group went back to bring more settlers leaving only two hundred behind. Whether by Indian attacks or disease, they dwindled until only a few were left and in an effort to protect themselves they migrated from Alabama up into Georgia until they reached Fort Mountain. Prince Modoc, who had remained behind with his people, ordered them to build a fort which would afford more permanent protection. For weeks they must have patiently carried the stones until finally their European-style line of defense, unlike the wooden stockades of the later English settlers, was completed on the flank of the mountain.

Now they were protected, for the outposts of fire pits illumined the night and any invaders were silhouetted against the sky. Moccasined feet or bare feet would become bloody feet in crossing the barrier of sharp stones which lay in front of the wall and the movement of rocks underfoot ruled out an attack by stealth. After lighting the fires, the Welsh could fall back among the trees and pick off their attackers as they crossed the rocks in the light from the flames.

How long they were able to survive among the Indians is not known, but stories about them and their blue eyes and golden hair continue to echo down through the centuries. Frank thought about how much we rely upon books forgetting those mysterious, mist covered eons before there were written records when the only history of a people's past came down to each successive generation through the memorized stories of the elders of a tribe. They alone transmitted stories of a "great wind" probably a hurricane, a devastating volcanic eruption, the disappearance of an island and its people into the ocean, a great victory in battle, and the deeds of heroic men and women.

Then he thought about another explanation for the wall—the story that de Soto and his men had built it as they hunted for gold on their journey through the southeast. De Soto was here in 1540 but according to what Frank had read about the period, the Spaniard's diaries indicated that they seem to have been in the area near Fort Mountain only about two weeks. Building walls was not the sort of work Spaniards liked and although de Soto would probably have used enforced Indian labor, he was an impatient man and gold was his real objective. This meant constant travel and a stone wall of defense would not have served any real purpose for him. When he interrogated the Indians about gold they often pointed toward the high mountains of Tennessee and North Carolina in an attempt to hurry the Spaniards on their way.

Just after sunset, Meg and Sarah returned from their explorations and water was heated for coffee. Meg had packed sandwiches and made a cake. Sarah found a flat, sheltered place to put her sleeping bag and lay down soon after dark. When Meg and Frank checked on her, the child's blond head rested against the large brown teddy bear she always cuddled at home and her breathing was soft and even. She was almost seven and very mature in some ways, but in others, perhaps, too imaginative, thought Frank. He hoped she would grow out of this fantasizing. At least tonight he would have a good night's sleep. He was emotionally exhausted by the week he had been through and tomorrow he would enjoy sharing his knowledge of the history of the wall with Sarah and Meg.

It was almost midnight when Sarah waked to the rhythmic tones of distant drums. They aren't like the drums I've heard in a parade, she thought. They are almost like notes of music, but somehow, the sound seems old and covered up with moss. The drums grew louder. Sarah put on her shoes and her coat and started in the direction of the strange poly-phony.

To her delight, she saw fireflies out in the for-est over near the wall. She loved chasing them in the summer but this was October and all the fireflies at home in Atlanta were gone. As she drew closer she saw that the flickers of light were not fireflies at all but torches and as they were carried along toward the wall, trees momentarily blocking them from view made them appear to flicker.

Then coming up in the east and in a trajectory with the wall was a light, a huge, pale yellowish-white incandescence, round and so immense she could see the dark places on the surface. It was the largest full moon she had ever seen.

It was almost as bright as if it were just after sunset and about a hundred yards away from her she could see figures wearing animal skins. They reminded her of the cave men pictures she had seen in a book but they weren't all rough and hairy look-ing. Their hair shone as blond in the moonlight as her own and their limbs were white skinned. Now the figures were climbing the wall and walking with a measured tread toward the full moon. Their arms were raised as if in worship and she stood watching hypnotized for it seemed the moon was pulling them toward it.

Then she realized that if she didn't hurry, they would all be gone before she could even speak to one of them! Sarah broke into a run. She had nearly reached the wall when her foot stepped on a loose rock and she tumbled forward hurting her knees and scraping her arms in an effort to protect her face.

When she looked up, she saw the last of the torches flickering out in the darkness like fireflies carried off by the wind. The notes of the drums had ceased.

On Sunday morning Frank Willard waked up feeling greatly refreshed. Soft golden rays of the morning sun sifted through the trees, birds were singing and in every way, it was a brand new day.

He looked over at his family. Meg was just waking up and greeted him with a sleepy smile, but Sarah who was usually up before anyone else lay still in her sleeping bag. Looking at her he couldn't even tell whether she was breathing she seemed in such a deep sleep and for a moment he was worried. He bent over and touched her shoulder.

"Honey, honey. Wake up."

"Who are you!" she cried out.

"What do you mean, who am I, I'm your father."

"Of course, Dad. I know you are. I guess I was just sound asleep." Her father laughed and ruffled the golden waves of her hair with his hand.

Sarah stretched and discovered to her suprise how sore her knees were. Stealing a cautious look at them, she saw they were badly scratched and that where the skin was broken some places were streaked with blood. Her parents would see this if she wore the shorts she had on the day before.

"Daddy, I want to tell you what. . . ." And then she suddenly stopped.

"Yes?"

"Nothing. Nothing important."

She remembered how her father had cut her off the morning before when she began talking about the beautiful music she had heard in the old cabin. Describing what she had seen at the wall might only irritate him. Then he would make her feel foolish by saying she was too imaginative. Sarah reached into her canvas pack and pulled out the pair of blue jeans to cover her injured knees. She would not tell him about the people on the wall—at least not now and maybe never.

The Woman in Black

Smoky Mountains, Tennessee

At first Ila Jeffers thought she was feverish and puny feeling because of the birthin' of Ginny Sue. She was glad midwife, Granny Moss, had come back by the house to check on her and felt all the more grateful since they lived aways up in the cove. Granny had been delivering babies nigh on to thirty years.

The midwife turned up the kerosene lamp and her knowledgeable eyes stared hard at Ila who lay there in the iron bed, her face white as the muslin sheet, her beautiful, shoulder length, silky black hair uncombed and tangled. Granny was worried.

"Your color ain't good, honey. I was lookin' to find you just as chipper as you were after your last young 'un. 'Member how when I come by here 'spectin' to see you lyin' up in the bed and you was out puttin' in taters' the very next afternoon?" Ila

64

nodded weakly and searched Granny Moss's eyes trying to fathom whatever secrets were contained in their green depths. Granny untied a bandana and some small, clear drugstore vials tumbled out, but they didn't contain pills they held herbs.

"I want you to take just a smidgen of this in a cup 'a hot tea every hour, Ila. This is the strongest yarb I ever seed and I was carrying some over the mountain to Nell Lyons, but there's enough for the both of you." Granny put a pinch of the "yarb" in a cup, went over and got the kettle off the top of the wood heater and poured in some hot water. When the liquid in the cup had turned a smoky yellow she handed it to Ila placing one arm behind the slim shoulders to help her sit up.

"Would you fetch Ginny Sue for me, Granny. I hear her fussin'. It's time I was nursin' her." Granny went over to the walnut cradle near the stone fireplace and as she picked up the small bundle, wrapped first in an old flour sack and then in a tiny handwoven wool kiver, the baby grew quiet in her practiced hands.

"I remember layin' Andrew in that cradle twenty-eight years ago. Where is that rascal?"

"Gone into town to buy me some aspirin."

"You shore he didn't go after no white lightnin'?"

"N'om. You know Andrew. He don't drink nor cuss. He's as good a man as a woman ever had." Granny pressed her thin lips together and her head bobbed up and down in agreement.

"That's true. I never heared nothin' but good of Andrew, and he shore were tickled 'bout this little girl. Just walked backards and forards with her in his arms, wantin' to hold her all the time 'til I had to tell him if she war' a little kitten all that handlin' would kill her."

"Granny, what's the matter with Ginny Sue? She's not nursin' good. She's fussin' like she's hungry but turnin' her head away."

"She shouldn't be a'doin' that."

"I'm scared, Granny. You reckon my baby's sick, too?" Ila's blue eyes had tears in them and her lower lip trembled.

"I don't know, Ila, but I'll be back this way tomorrow afternoon and I'll look in on ye and the baby."

"Ef it don't discomfit ye none, Granny." Ila looked up at her gratefully.

Granny hadn't gone over a mile before she met Andrew in his pick-up truck. He waved to her to stop and she pulled her old blue Plymouth toward the outside of the one lane road while he parked close to the mountainside. He read her face.

"She's bad off, ain't she Granny?"

His eyes looked anguished, then the line of his jaw hardened and he shook his head.

"It's chancy. We'll just have to wait and see."

"Yes, wait and see."

"Now, if you could get Dr. Curry to come up here."

"I went by his place. He's gone to Asheville and won't be back until late tomorrow afternoon. Can't you help her any?"

"I left her some of my medicine, Andy. I'm goin' to stop to see Ila on my way back from Union

Camp area." But she didn't get back the next day because Nell Lyons went into labor and the baby didn't arrive until late that night. She stayed on at the Lyons's house two more days which Granny almost never did, but Nell was quite weak. Will Lyons was mighty good with cattle but he didn't know much about how to help take care of a new baby.

The morning after Granny left, Will was down at the barn before daylight milking the cows. As it began to grow light he was surprised to see the slim figure of a woman in a black dress silhouetted against the doorway of the barn. Her features were not visible in the semi-darkness and there was nothing familiar about her appearance. When he spoke she held her head down and made no reply. Then she was standing beside him and noticing the woman had a cup in her hand, he asked her if she would like some milk. She held it out to be filled but left without thanking him or saying a word. Early next morning at about the same time, she came into the barn once more.

"Good morning," he said, but she did not reply. Once more he filled her cup and he thought he saw her nod gratefully, but she still did not speak. Blackberry winter was what the mountain folk called this unseasonably cold weather in May and because of that he took notice that she did not have a coat on over her dress. He told Nell about it when he went back to the house and she said it might be one of the neighbor girls come over because their cow had gone dry.

At the little cabin on the other side of the mountain, Ila seemed to be a little stronger the evening after Granny Moss had left her the herbs. Andrew prepared steaming hot tea for her and each time when she drank it she would say she felt better. The baby, however, was still not nursing the way she had at first and his wife thought Andrew should fetch the doctor as soon as he returned. By morning Ila, herself, had taken a turn for the worse. She was flushed and feverish, tossing, moaning and too delirious even to hold her baby, Ginny, who now lay listlessly in the cradle.

Why wasn't Granny Moss back? That morning Andrew drove down the road a piece thinking he might see her and make sure she came up to the cabin, but there was no sign of Granny. When he returned he first thought his wife was asleep, then he realized she was dead. Within an hour the baby girl gave a little cry and breathed her last. Then great, harsh sobs began to rack his thin shoulders and he flung himself across the bed beside his dead wife. He must have fallen asleep for the next thing he knew someone was pounding on the door.

It was Granny Moss and the doctor.

"Andrew, I thought that wife of your'n needed him so I went back by way of his house and brought him, how is. . . ."

"You're too late."

She saw the agony on his face and fell silent. Andrew stepped back to let them in. The doctor went over to the bed first, looked down at Ila and didn't even bother to take her pulse.

"Where's the baby, Andrew?"

"Hit's in the crib."

He picked up the limp little form and then, very gently, laid her back in the cradle. I doubt I could have done anything even if I'd been here. Everbody that's had this fever has been mighty sick with it, and I thought we'd lose more folks than we did. Andrew, I'm sorry as I can be."

The funeral was held the next afternoon in the little cemetery on top of a nearby hill. Blackberry winter was still here and a cold, gray day it was, with a mizzling sort of rain. It put Andrew in mind of the day of his father's funeral the winter before; how Ila had stood next to him strong and comforting but now, she too was gone and he was all alone. The loss of the baby hurt for they had looked forward to it together, but he had never suffered anything like the pain he felt over losing Ila.

"Oh death where is thy sting, oh grave where is thy victory . . ." the preacher's voice intoned and as he heard those words pronounced to comfort so many over the years, a vast rage engulfed him. He knew Ila and their child were in heaven and beyond any more suffering—but what about him? Didn't God care anything about him? What did he, Andrew, have left! He had never felt as close to the Lord as his wife had always seemed to be and today—not at all. Andrew raised the collar of his overcoat up around his neck to shield himself from the wind; but the worst chill of all was inside him and it took every ounce of his determination to keep from shaking. Lord, he felt like he was freezing to death and it was inside him.

Will and Nell Lyons talked about how sad it was and how bad Andrew was looking.

"Time's a great healer, Will," said his wife and Will wondered how some women always had a saying to cover things no matter how bad they were. And then he remembered that even after the harshest winter, ice melts, there are warm breezes, trees bloom, spring comes. Maybe his wife was right.

Next morning he was going about his milking and when the cow turned her head and mooed, he looked in that direction. There came the girl dressed in black and she was holding out the cup just as she had done on the other two occasions.

"Good-morning," he said cheerfully, but no reply came. He didn't try to talk to her any more and she stood there without a word while the only sound was that of the warm, fresh milk spurting and the ping as it hit the inside of the tin cup. He decided that this morning he was going to follow her at a distance and see if he could find out where she went. As she left the barn he rose from his milking stool and quietly walked after her. It was a pewter gray sky now instead of black and he could see the dark, slim form seemingly glide along ahead of him as they crossed the pasture, he about fifty feet behind her. On she went through the brush around the side of Big Bear Mountain with Will following. He worried that a careless step along the path might start some of the small, loose rocks rolling and he would be discovered.

The sun would be up in a few minutes and then, if she looked back, she would surely see him for now they emerged from the woods. She took the muddy little road that led up the back way to the top of the hill and walked at such a pace that Will could scarcely keep up with her, but by now he knew her destination. This was the road the gravediggers sometimes used and across the top of the hill was the community cemetery. For the first time he began to feel uneasy. Why was she on her way to the graveyard?

He was surprised to see the cemetery gate standing half open and through it she went, only stopping to pull it closed behind her. He thought then she would see him for certain but although she turned and was facing him, she didn't appear to be aware of his presence. He followed her only a few feet further and then stopped hidden from view behind a large tulip poplar. As he watched, the girl walked over to a grave and as he peered between the stones, she vanished. Shocked and incredulous, Will still did not doubt what he had seen. On the way home, and this time he took the main road, he saw Jake Jackson rattling along in his old truck. He hailed him.

"I'm on my way to set out a load of new Christmas tree seedlings. You want to help?"

"Jake, I need help myself. How about turning around."

"I got work to do. Where you want to go?"

"To the cemetery."

"Cemetery!"

"Yes. You got a shovel on this truck?"

"Sure do." Something in Will's expression made him turn around and they headed up the hill. When they reached the graveyard, Will went around to the back of the truck and got the shovel. "Can you find another?"

"Just this small one."

"Well, bring it along." He led the way over to a freshly dug grave at the edge of the cemetery.

"Why this is Ila Jeffer's grave. She died of the fever only a few days ago. We can't go diggin' her up."

"I got good reason for this, Jake. Now, don't be squeamish and just give me a hand." As the hole grew wider and deeper they began to hear a faint sound. They dug faster, throwing the dirt up furiously around the edge of the grave. The sound grew louder and became a whimper punctuated by cries. When they reached the coffin, Will knelt down and tore the lid clean off. There in the coffin lay Ila Jeffers in a black dress but she was not alone. In the crook of one arm rested her baby.

"Lord, a mighty! This baby's alive," cried out Will. The baby was crying and those were the sounds the men had heard as they were digging. Will reached into the coffin to pick up the baby and as he did, his fingers touched something else. Beside the mother's hand was the metal milk cup he had filled that morning.

Andrew Jeffers had not built a fire nor had a bite to eat for two days. His girl, Cindy, who had been visiting her aunt in West Virginia had come home the night before and been pressing him to eat some of the food folks had brought. He was about to leave the little cabin to cut fresh wood for the stove when he saw a truck heading up the road toward his house. His hand reached for his shotgun when his daughter spoke up. "Quit that, Daddy. It's Mr. Jackson's truck." Then he recognized it as the Jackson Tree Farm truck. The men drove up near the porch and when Andrew went out and heard the cries of a baby, he thought they were up to some kind of strange carrying on, and his face grew red with anger.

"Wait, before you holler at us, Andy. We ain't meanin' to hurt you none," said Will Lyons. "We've brought something for you. This is your own baby.

Don't tell me how bad the Lord's done treated you now."

It was a miracle, a real miracle, said everyone. And the story of the mother whose spirit somehow managed to return to care for her baby can still be heard in that part of the Tennessee mountains not far from the North Carolina line.

Laura

Campbellsville, Kentucky

The afternoon was gray and misty, not the kind that Larry Huff would usually choose for a motorcycle ride. But he had just traded in his old motorcycle for a new Honda—bought himself a new jacket—and the temptation to take off was irresistible.

When he sped down Highway 55 out of Campbellsville, Kentucky, and headed south toward Columbia, he had no premonition of what lay in store for him.

It was a great ride, with the cool, moist air blowing in his face as he swooped around the curves. There were almost no cars on the road. In fact, he must have gone five miles before he met one. In some places the fog made it difficult to see for any distance ahead but there were often foggy places along this road and Larry didn't really mind. It gave him a feeling of being in another world—a world of fluffy whiteness and, above all, quiet. He liked that, for in the small house where he lived with his parents and four brothers and sisters, there was often so much noise that there was no chance to think. He wasn't sure just what it was that he wanted to be alone to think about, but sometimes he grew angry inside when the clamor of voices made his thoughts so jerky that he couldn't make sense out of whatever was gnawing on him at the moment. He could put things together when he rode alone like this.

Instead of the weather clearing, a slow, drizzling rain began to fall, but Larry still did not want to turn back. As he rounded one of the curves, a small, single tree near a clump of trees on his right appeared to move. But when he approached, he saw it was a thin-looking girl wearing a cloak walking beside the road.

He stopped to ask if there was anything he could do for her, she looked so cold and forlorn, her hair clinging wetly about her cheeks, her dress long and bedraggled. At first he thought she was not going to answer, but she replied, "Well, if you don't mind, I'd like to have a ride down the road a piece to my house." By now the drizzle had changed to a light rain and Larry offered her his new jacket. She put it on gratefully and climbed up behind him on the motorcycle, winding her arms about his waist. He was conscious of the cold from her hands penetrating even through his shirt. The ride was not a comfortable one as her grip gradually grew tighter, and his back felt cold as ice.

They were near Cane Valley when she spoke
up and pointed to a house set back from the highway. "That's where I live," she said and Larry
turned up the road toward it. It was an old farm-

house and the girl muttered a quick, "Thank you," ran up the front steps and in the door, closing it behind her. Larry was so glad not to have her holding on with those cold hands around his waist that he hurriedly took off.

It was not until he was part way home that he remembered his new jacket, but by then it was getting quite dark and he had no desire to return to the farmhouse at night.

Next morning he headed back down Highway 55 toward Cane Valley and when he reached the

girl's house he went up and knocked on the front door, thinking she might answer it. A woman came to the door instead, so he described the girl and said he had lent her his jacket.

The woman's eyes filled with tears. "I don't know how you've done it. You've described just how my girl, Laura, looked, but she's been dead seven years."

Larry stared at her in disbelief. "Ma'am, I just can't believe it. She was as real as can be and I could even feel how wet and cold she was."

"Wait a minute. I'd like for you to go with me," said the woman. She went into the house and got her coat and he followed her to the back and up to the top of a hill where there was a small family cemetery surrounded by a fence. As she opened the gate, he was surprised to see something was hanging over the top of a tombstone on the far side.

When they reached it he was amazed. His jacket was draped over the tombstone and below it, engraved on the stone, was the name "Laura." The date was seven years ago. He reclaimed the jacket but it was too damp to put on, even if he had wanted to.

Although he kept the coat for several years, he never seemed able to wear it, for always, after he had worn it for a few minutes, it would begin to feel cold and wet and he would have to take it off. The jacket still looked like new but finally one night, after trying again to wear it, he became angry and threw it in the fire.

A strange odor suffused the room like the scent of flowers massed around a freshly dug grave. Larry was so terrified he ran out of the house into the night.

Even now as he tells the story, his face turns white, his eyes fill with horror and he will never ride down Highway 55 on a foggy, rainy day again.

The Coming of the Demon

Middleway, West Virginia

Adam Livingstone was an honest, religious man and a hard-working farmer. It is hard to realize how a man like this can become involved with a demon, and yet that is what happened.

Near the beginning of the nineteenth century Livingstone and his wife came down to what later became West Virginia from Pennsylvania and purchased a lakeside farm near the town that is now Middleway. It was then called Smithfield and later Wizard Clip. This last name came from the series of disasters that happened to the Livingstone family.

In front of their farm and beside the Opequon River ran the wagon route from Baltimore to southwest Virginia, Kentucky, and Tennessee. During the day, wagon after wagon rattled along the road and Livingstone would sell or barter his farm produce with the wagon drivers.

One bitterly cold November night the event befell the Livingstones that was to lead to a terrifying series of happenings, although it appeared quite commonplace at the time. During these days there were few inns with accommodations for travelers and they often stopped at a house and asked if they might spend the night.

The Livingstones were in bed listening to the rain and wind outside when they heard a pounding on their front door. Adam went down to see who it could be. He cautiously opened the door a few inches but the force of the wind was such that it tore the door from his hand and flung it open revealing a black hole in the outer darkness. In the midst of it stood a tall stranger, his cloak billowing in the wind.

"My wagon wheel is broken and I am not able to have it repaired until morning," said the stranger. "I would like to ask for a night's lodging, sir, and I assure you I will pay you generously."

"We have an extra room and you are welcome to it," replied Livingstone. "My wife has gone to bed or I would ask her to prepare food for you, but let me show you to your room."

The stranger appeared grateful and followed him up the steep, winding stairs to a room which was sparsely furnished but had a comfortable feather bed. Although he wore the clothes of a gentleman, Livingstone took his usual precaution of locking the door at the foot of the stairs. This was a common practice when a family lodged strangers on the second floor for the night.

The Livingstones heard the man walk about the room. They heard his boots hit the floor one by one and then the bed creaked. Leaving only the candle burning by their bed, they were soon asleep. A short time later they were awakened by the sound of a terrible moaning and groaning above them, punctuated now and then by a sharp outcry of pain. It was the traveler.

Taking the bedside candle, Livingstone unlocked the door to the stairs and went up to see what was the matter. He found his guest tossing in his bed and deathly ill. The man told him he did not expect to live to see daylight, and he asked if Livingstone would summon a Catholic priest to give him the last rites, admitting that he had neglected his

religion in health but now felt need of its consolation.

Livingstone told him that there was no priest nearby nor could he hope to find one closer than Maryland but that he would ask his neighbors, the McSherrys and the Minghinis, who were Catholic and perhaps they could tell him of one. Mrs. Livingstone had come up, and as she listened to the conversation she began to grow angry.

"Surely, you are not going out on any such wild-goose chase on a night like this. The best thing we can do is go back to bed, and I'll wager this guest of ours will be as well as you or I by morning."

But the Livingstones could not sleep the rest of the night, for there were the most pitiful cries and pleas coming from the room above. Finally, just before day came, all was quiet. About eight o'clock when they heard no sound, Livingstone went up. Their guest was dead. It was then that they realized they did not know his name and couldn't find it in any of his belongings. Mrs. Livingstone told the neighbors a traveler had asked to lodge with them the night before and had died in his sleep. She did not mention his begging them to summon a priest. The funeral was a simple one, held late the following afternoon.

After the Livingstones returned to their home, Adam built a fire and they sat down before it to warm themselves. Suddenly, the logs in the fireplace began to writhe and twist so violently that they erupted from the fireplace into a fiery dance around the room. Livingstone ran from one to the other trying to catch them and put them back but as soon as he did they would fly out again. When the dancing finally stopped, the Livingstones were too frightened to sleep.

Tired as Livingstone was, he went down to the road with some of his produce the next morning and was surprised to hear a wagon driver cursing at him. The man's team of oxen had stopped in the middle of the road.

"Take that rope down! What are you doing, tying a rope across a public road?" the angry man shouted. The exhausted and bewildered Livingstone could see no rope at all and thought the man must be drunk. The driver took out a large knife and began slashing the air with it. To his amazement the knife met no resistance. Livingstone suggested that he drive on. He did and the wagon went through. What a shame for a man to be drunk so early in the day, thought Livingstone. It was only a short time, however, before another wagon came clattering down the road with a load of pots and pans and the same thing happened. The driver pulled to a stop so quickly that several of the pans fell banging and rattling to the ground. Then he started to shout about a rope, and shook his fist at Livingstone. Finally, he was persuaded to drive on, but similar incidents kept up for several weeks.

By now the Livingstones and their neighbors, who had all noticed these strange events, were sure that they were the work of some supernatural power. Each day brought new and frightening phenomena. Showers of stones would strike the Livingstone house, articles of furniture would topple over, balls of fire rolled over the floor without any apparent cause. But most frequent was a sharp clipping noise as if made by gigantic, invisible shears which could be heard in and around the house, and crescent shaped slits began to appear in the family clothes and table linen.

Mrs. Livingstone and a lady visitor were sitting on the porch talking and the lady commented on the fine flock of ducks waddling through the yard on the way to the river. She had no sooner spoken than the uncanny, invisible shears went "Clip-clip, clip-clip!" and one after another each duck's head fell to the ground before the horrified ladies' eyes.

The young men of the neighborhood talked Livingstone into letting them hold a dance at his home. One boastful fellow brought his rifle and bragged about all he would do if "the Clipper" came near him. For a while everything went smoothly, but right in the middle of one of the dances the fellow who had been boasting began yelling wildly. There was the sound of huge, demoniacal scissors whacking through cloth. The boaster grasped his britches which were now flapping around the back of his legs and ran through the nearest door.

That night, after the dance was over, Livingstone had a strange dream. He dreamed he was standing at the foot of a hill looking up at a man in flowing black robes who was conducting a religious ceremony. As he watched, a voice spoke saying, "I am the man who can rid you of the demon." He was much astonished and decided the man in his dream was a priest so he decided to attend Catholic services nearby at Sheperdstown. He went with his Catholic neighbors, and the moment he saw the

After the demon arrived, the field behind the Livingstone home seemed always to be shrouded in fog.

priest he recognized the man he had seen in his dream.

Tears streaming down this face, he poured out the story of his heartless treatment of the stranger, the weird chain of events that had followed, and he begged for help. Father Cahill was a big-fisted Irishman who was not afraid of the devil himself and he accompanied Livingstone back home. There he got down on his knees and prayed, and sprinkled holy water on the threshold of the house.

"Now, I want you to take me to the place where the stranger was buried," said the priest, and together they went to an old cemetery. Livingstone showed him the grave and the priest began to consecrate it. As he did so, the wind rose, leaves rustled, and small trees started to sway. But along with the wind sounds there was another that grew and swelled until it became a dreadful sort of moan. Livingstone was terribly frightened. He looked at the dark waters of the nearby lake tossing tumultuously. In a few minutes the moan faded and the waters grew still, perhaps, because they had taken back their own.

After that day, there were no more signs of the demon at the Livingstone home, and Adam Livingstone was so grateful that he deeded thirty-four acres of his farm to the Catholic church. The deed may be seen today, recorded on the yellowing pages of an old book in the County Clerk's office at Charles Town, West Virginia. The land is a half mile or so west of the main turnpike through Middleway. The soil is poor, and shattered limestone rock is close to the surface. For many years the foundation of an ancient house could be seen. Many have claimed to hear the hoof beats of a galloping horse there, and on dark and blustery autumn nights they talk of a figure in a billowing cape striding toward the small chapel, built on the spot by the Catholic church, and disappearing within. Is it the spirit of the stranger returning to give thanks at being released from this earth by the priest? No one really knows.

The Letter

South Mountain, Maryland

James Ramsay stood in the fading sunlight. He was surrounded by the bodies of the Confederate dead and, who knows, perhaps their spirits. The battle of South Mountain was over, for the Confederates had come out of a thin line of woods scarcely two hours before, helpless and with empty muskets. His own New York regiment, taking cruel advantage of the situation, had shot them down as they stood there not twenty feet away.

Most of the dead Confederates were from the coastal district of North Carolina. They wore "butternut" uniforms, the color ranging all the way from deep coffee-brown to the whitish brown of ordinary dust. He looked down into the poor, pinched faces, worn with marching and scant fare and his anger toward them died. There was no "secession" in those rigid forms nor in those fixed

eyes staring blankly at the sky. It was not "their" war anymore.

Some of the Union soldiers were taking the finer powder from the cartridge boxes of the dead and priming their muskets with it. Except for that, each body lay untouched as it had fallen. Darkness came on quickly before there was time to bury the dead. Ramsay and his comrades unrolled the blankets of the rebels and went about covering each body. The air was full of the fragrance of pennyroyal, an herb bruised by the tramping of a hundred feet, and he would always remember it as part of this day.

It was Sunday, September 14, 1862, but the air was chilly, and after munching on some of their cooked rations and listening to the firing which continued until about nine o'clock that evening, the men drew their blankets over them and went to sleep. It was a strange sight, thought Ramsay. Stretched out here in the narrow field lay living Yankee and dead Confederate, side by side, nor could one be told from the other.

Sometime after midnight, James Ramsay awoke very thirsty. He reached for his water flask to find it empty, and then he recalled that he had forgotten to fill it at the stream. He must have said this aloud to himself for the figure next to him rose on one elbow and extended his own water flask. Ramsay drank from it gratefully, thanked him, and was about to lie back upon his arms when a voice said, "I have a letter in my breast pocket. Would you see that it gets to my wife?"

"Of course," replied Ramsay, and exhausted he fell asleep once more. He awoke at daylight as he

had for so many dawns during the past few months and began to recall where he was and what had happened the day before while he waited for the rest of the camp to stir. Then he remembered his buddy next to him who had given him a drink during the night. What was it the man had said? He had asked him to carry a letter to his wife, that was it. Poor fellow. Like all of them, he knew that each day might so easily be his last. Ramsay glanced over at him curiously to see who it was.

Then he realized that the man on his right was not from his own regiment but was one of the dead Confederates they had not had time to bury the night before. It must be the fellow asleep on the other side, then. He turned. This, too, was a dead Confederate. Nor was there any water flask on the body.

He could not believe his eyes. He was certain it had been no dream for he clearly remembered the man raising up to give him water. One thing would tell him. He peeled the blanket back from the Confederate and reached into his breast pocket. In it was a letter addressed to "Mrs. John Carpenter." He opened it and began to read: "My dearest wife, I think of you daily and in the event I am not able to return to tell you. I want you to know that . . ."

Ramsay read no further. He was not a superstitious man, but he knew that his experience was too real to discount. He would never forget the night he had met the spirit of a Confederate soldier named John Carpenter as they slept side by side in a field in Maryland.

The Ghost Fiddlers

Hill Country, West Virginia

There is an old house in West Virginia that only comes alive at night. That is, if you can say that a house inhabited by spirits can come "alive."

The old log cabin leaned forward and seemed to stare menacingly. Its supports sagged. A door hung from one hinge. The young couple stood for a moment and stared back. Then the man walked over to look at the steps.

"Pretty good shape. This 'uns a house with good timber and we can make it right."

"Oh, Peter, this old house scares me just to look at it."

"Scares you?"

"Yes, there's something wrong about it. There'll never be anything but sadness in it."

"You're not thinkin' straight, Sarry. Yer family lets the tunes from all that fiddlin' make 'em feel all

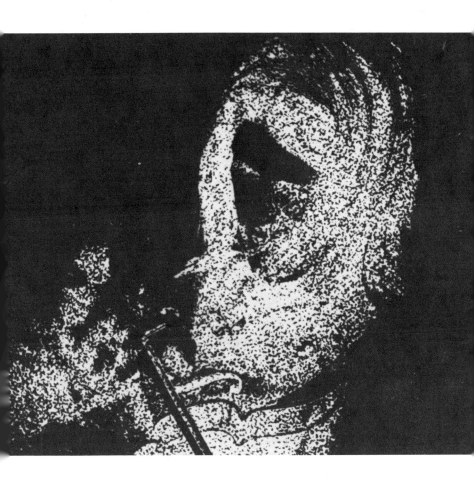

sorts a crazy things. Now, remember, I don't never want none of that fiddlin' in our home."

Sarry's eyes looked hurt, but she gave a reluctant little nod. She was a pretty girl who loved to sing and dance, and she was from a family of fiddle players. The girls could play about as well as the men. But Peter Barton thought the fiddle was an instrument of the devil, for that's the way he was raised. Music led a body away from things they ought to be doing, like serving the Lord, and could make him forget he would soon be standing before the judgment seat.

Peter had wanted to preach but had worked so hard there was no time to practice at it. But my, what a powerful prayer he could make! Lots of folks went to preachin' just to hear Peter Barton pray.

He began to repair the house and sometimes Sarry would come out bringing some of the yellow rosebushes from her homeplace to plant to keep it from looking so desolate.

It was a somber wedding with no music, for Sarry's dad and brothers knew better than to fetch any fiddles along. A year later a boy was born. Peter wanted to call him after one of the thundering prophets of the Old Testament, but Sarry said her grandpappy's name, James, was the same as one of the apostles' and her husband agreed. They lived to themselves, for Peter never wanted to take her over to see her family, for that instrument of the devil, the fiddle, could often be heard, its strains floating from the cabin at night. Secretly, Peter feared he might come to like one of the gay tunes or plaintive lover's ballads and then he was convinced he would lose his faith.

Folks passing the Barton house at suppertime could hear Peter's strong, resonant voice reciting the blessing as if he were giving a benediction to the multitude. He took Sarry and the boy to church and never missed a meeting. People said the prayers he prayed could make chills run down a man's spine.

Somehow, he never had any close friends, for he
didn't seem to trust anybody. Some said it was
because he'd had to scrabble so hard for what he'd
got. They also said he was a strong-tempered man
and that both Sarry and the boy were afraid of him.

Sarry's ma took sick one day and they sent for
Sarry, so Peter took her and the boy, James, on their
two white mules. Right off, James saw a fiddle
hanging on the wall and asked his granddaddy what
it was for. It was the first time he'd ever seen one.
His granddaddy took it down and played a gay, lilt-
ing melody. James wanted to try it but his father
scowled and the boy was afraid to touch it. When
they left, Peter told James that he was never to play
such an instrument of the devil and if he ever took it
up, he'd have to leave home.

Sometimes Peter would make money by running a raft of logs down the river. There was much
timber in the area and he would tie the loose logs
into the raft and ride it downstream where he
would sell them to buy land. It took about four days
because he would have to walk back. One day while
he was gone, James's grandmother became sick
again and he and his mother went over to the
house. He asked his granddad to play for him, and
when he had finished James wanted to try it. Sarry's
father suggested she take the fiddle home with her
and teach the boy while his father was away.

Sarry looked at the fiddle with longing and all
the beautiful, haunting melodies she had learned as
a girl came to mind. How she had missed them! She
couldn't resist, and from then on she and James
would play when his father was away.

One morning Peter told them good-by and set out for the river to run a raft of logs downstream and sell the timber.

"The water's pretty high, Sarry, and it may take me longer to get back, for some of the small streams are going to get higher if it rains some more. I may have trouble gettin' acrost them on foot, but I'm aimin' to get back in about four days."

Sarry did her chores. James chopped some wood, planted taters in the garden, and it was late afternoon when he finished. That night after supper his mother saw him look up toward the loft where they had the fiddle hidden. Her eyes met his and she nodded her head, "Go ahead, Jamie." He played while his mother sat listening in the old rocking chair her Pa had given her. Every now and then she would take the fiddle herself and play a tune. The two of them had such a good time they paid no mind to the late hour.

Meanwhile, Peter had set out down the river but the water was high, and about ten miles from home he reached a spot where the river narrowed and curved. Here the current was swift and it pulled the raft right over the big rocks he had always managed to see and avoid when the water was lower. The raft went all to pieces and only by clinging to one of the logs was he able to keep from drowning. He stopped at a house to dry himself and by the time he had walked all the way home, it was getting on toward midnight. He was surprised to see the light of a lamp burning in the little cabin, but as he drew closer he knew why. The wind brought the sound of a gay, foot-tapping melody called

"Sweet Sunny Sal." Peter's face grew grim and hard. The appealing lilt of the tune, rather than touch his heart, only moved him to anger.

A fiddle was used at dances and other frolics. It was clearly the instrument of the devil in the eyes of the mountain preachers, and Peter flung open the door in a black rage. He snatched the fiddle out of Jamie's hands and taking his knife he deliberately cut every string. Then he hung it near the mantel and turned to Jamie, thundering, "There hangs the instrument of the devil as a reminder to all them who would not obey. I told you, Jamie, you'd have to leave this house if you ever brought a fiddle into it. Now, you go to your grandpappy's and stay there."

Jamie had no light, but he was afraid of his father and he left right then. Sarry thought he would go to her Pa's place and stay there 'til Peter cooled down and then come back. But that was not to be.

The following morning Peter rose early to milk the cow. She was in the far pasture and when he went to fetch her, he saw a dark crumpled figure lying at the foot of the cliff at one side of the field. It was Jamie. He had lost his footing in the dark, fallen down the cliff head first, and struck a stump. The boy's neck was broken. Peter carried his son's body back to the house.

It is said that Peter was never the same. He no longer took his logs down the river. He scarcely talked to anyone now, and in church he never prayed aloud again. Four years later he was killed when one of the mules kicked him, splitting his head open. Some folks said he had told Sarry he would live only four years, one year for each string he had cut on the fiddle. He was buried beside his son in the graveyard.

Sarry lived on at the house getting queerer and queerer, and late at night when folks walked the path near the cabin they would hear the strains of a fiddle playing. One morning someone found her sitting in her rocking chair with a fiddle across her

lap and a smile upon her face. Stranger still, even after the old lady died, the sounds kept on and, if anything, there were more and more reports of music rippling through the night air coming from the old cabin, sometimes gay but more often sad and plaintive.

Even today there are few people who care to walk the path near the old cabin after dark, nor does anyone want to stay over night or live there again. It is a dark, sagging skeleton of a place. Yet they say that near midnight the eerie, haunting music of Jamie's fiddle may still be heard—coming from beyond the grave.

The Haunted Copper Mine

Ducktown, Tennessee

Jack McCaulla had worked in the mines all his life and, as his friends used to say, "There ain't much Jack's afeard of." Like every man who worked in the mines, Jack lived with danger, but he knew how to handle it better than most. Or so everyone thought.

The Ducktown copper mines were on the Georgia-Tennessee border and they were the only places a man could make money as good as a dollar a day in the 1890s.

Jack was working a tunnel about four hundred feet down one day when a bunch of men became scared to death. One of the engines failed that ran both the air pump, which pushed fresh air through

the mine, and the wooden elevator that brought men up from the shafts. The miners ran toward the shaft and began scurrying up the steel wire ladder that hung on the solid rock wall, climbing from level to level.

They were all crowded around the base of the ladder and some were pushing and shoving. Just as McCaulla's turn came to go up it, a panic-stricken old man thrust in ahead of him and McCaulla stood aside, letting him go up first. Jack was the last man to go up the ladder. Later his fellow miners talked about it, and when one of the mine officials asked him if it were true, he just said, "Well, we couldn't all climb that ladder at once. Someone always has to be last."

A few months later Jack McCaulla was working about four hundred feet down in the mine when he went to the end of one of the tunnels that had been blasted the day before in a pocket of rich copper-bearing ore. By the light of the lamp on his cap he began to pick up large chunks of the ore and load his mine car with the blasted-down rock.

He had been loading the car for almost an hour when he heard a peculiar hissing sound as if air were escaping from the pipe. The pipes brought the life-saving fresh air under heavy pressure along the tunnels. The sound grew louder and he began to think it might come from water running down the side of the tunnel. He stopped shoveling the ore and began to listen. As he did so he was aware of a change in the sound. No longer was it a hissing nor the noise of running water, but it was becoming more and more eerie.

It was a chorus sobbing and moaning in unison, and he recognized human voices. Somehow, he knew it was the voices of all the miners who had died in this mine and their cries were so loud they seemed to surround and overwhelm him. His hands became clammy, his face beaded with perspiration, and he didn't wait finish loading his mine car but pushed the car to the shaft as quickly as possible. The wailing seemed to follow him all the way to the skip. He rode the skip up, dumped his ore, and went to the surface boss and told him he had heard the cries of all the men who had ever been killed in this mine.

The face of the man who had long been unafraid was the color of ashes. The boss looked at him and paid him off, nor did McCaulla ever go back to work in the Isabella copper mine at Ducktown again.

The Ghost of John Henry Lives On

Talcott, West Virginia

Some people in Talcott, Hilldale, and Hinton, West Virginia, say the ghost of John Henry still haunts the east portal of the Big Bend Tunnel. And it is true that within days after John Henry's death, work came to a halt because laborers could still hear his hammers ringing in the tunnel.

In 1870, when the tunnel was started, John Henry was there. The tunnel was one of the most ambitious projects of its day. More than a mile long, it would cut off nine miles as it went through Big Bend Mountain and came out on the other side. The tunnel was a real man-eater, for the hard, red, shale rock through which it was driven would crumble when exposed to air and at least one out of every

108

five workers died from rock falls in the building of
it.

The steel drivers were the princes of the working crews, and John Henry was king of them all. He
was a big, black man, six feet tall, two hundred
pounds, superbly muscled, and an artist with his
hammers. It was not easy to slam one hammer at the
end of a 1 1/2-inch-diameter drill hour after hour,
day after day without missing.

Little Bill, John Henry's "turner" held the drill
turning it slightly after each blow giving it a little
shake to flip the rock dust out of the hole. The drills
would get dull after a few minutes and while those
hammers of John Henry's flew back and forth—he
could swing a hammer in each hand—Little Bill
would hold out a hand to the "walker" who kept getting the drills resharpened by the blacksmith at the
tunnel entrance, and he'd slip another into the hole
fast between hammer blows. The steel driver
couldn't break the rhythm of his hammers any
more than a distance runner could break his stride.

In rock drilling contests the drivers kept up a
rate of ninety blows a minute and a dozen times in a
fifteen-minute match. The "turner" would replace
the steel drill, with bloodied flesh to pay if his tim-
ing was poor.

But the most famous contest that ever happened was when John Henry told his boss he could
beat the steam drill. John Henry was proud man.
The rest of the men admired him and Banks Terry,
who used to do odd jobs in the tunnel, always talked
a lot about him—said he could drive steel straight
ahead or straight into the roof while standing on a

powder keg, never tiring, never missing a stroke, singing all the while and wearing out drills as fast as they were brought to him.

The steam drill had not been out long before John Henry thought he'd like to have a match with one.

So John Henry said to the captain:

"A man ain't nothing but a man,
But before I let that steam drill beat me
down,
I'll die with my hammers in my hands, Lord,
Lord,
Die with my hammers in my hands."

As his hammers flew back and forth ringing through the tunnel, John Henry's body glistened with sweat and shone as though it had been polished. The clang of his hammers was a high, steady chorus even above the sound of the steam drill as this giant of a man pitted himself against the machine. His boss and fellow workers stood watching. There had been some joking with John Henry before the match, but now everyone was silent.

For the first ten minutes the man and the steam drill seemed to be going at about the same pace. Then, little by little, John Henry began to pull ahead. There was one thing in his favor. Every so often the Burleigh drill would clog up on rock dust or hang up in a crack, and while the steam driller was taking care of this, John Henry went right on slinging those hammers—clang, clang, clang.

It was thirty-five minutes before the match was over and by that time John Henry had driven fourteen feet while the steam drill had driven only nine. John Henry turned to the steam driller and said, "Your hole's done choke and your drill done broke." The match was over and John Henry had won. But the big, proud, black man had trouble walking.

"I feel a roarin' and a rollin' in my head," he told Banks Terry, and he staggered home, laid down his hammers, and went to bed. The next morning he was dead. The feelings he had described are the classic symptoms of a stroke and few people nowadays, since the coming of power tools, can imagine such a brutal, man-killing contest.

Later, in 1876 a major rock fall killed a whole train crew, and a brick mason named Alfred Owens was one of those hired by the railroad to work in the tunnel and face it with brick. Owens had lived in the area all his life and been in the tunnel many a time as a boy. It was cold and damp inside it that November afternoon as he hurried to fit the last bricks into an arch and finish before he left. Only a half-dozen bricks remained when he heard a sound in the tunnel. A stray dog, a rat, or worse, a rock fall, for in the great dark voids above the brick arching, blocks of rock shifted and fell with frightening frequency.

He hurried to put the remaining bricks in place, but as he did so, another sound rang out—a clang, clang, clang, clang nearby—and as he looked down the tunnel he saw a shadowy figure in the orange light of his lamp. It was the outline of a huge, strapping man silhouetted near the tunnel opening. In each hand was a hammer and the

immense arms swung with smooth rapidity, never faltering, never losing their rhythm.

Owens was stunned. It was the entrance through which he had planned to leave. He edged toward it, pressing his back close against the tunnel wall while the loud clanging of the hammers striking steel went on and on. The air in the tunnel was cold, but Owens could feel perspiration running down his face. The palms of his hands were damp with fear. He became too frightened to move. A rock dislodged itself near his head and struck his shoulder, but even this did not frighten him nearly as much as the awesome figure swinging the hammers completely unmindful of him.

Then his foot slipped on the wet rock of the tunnel floor and he pitched forward almost at the very feet of—of what? An apparition? It could only be the specter of John Henry—once a living man with so much heart and so much brawn he had dared to take on a machine and conquer it. Now, he had returned to the scene of his triumph.

Owens shook with fear, but when he managed to look up, the figure was gone and the tunnel quiet. He was certain he had seen the ghost of John Henry. That night he sought out the old man Banks Terry. He described what had happened and Terry only nodded. Even now, some say that the ghost of John Henry still returns to haunt the Big Bend Tunnel. They say they have heard the sound of his hammers and that his shadowy form stalks along through the darkness, unmindful of the water that slowly drips from overhead to form long and eerie stalactites.

A Visitor from the Dead

Grant Town, West Virginia

Jessie Jackson was a pretty blond girl whose husband was a miner. But John never seemed satisfied to stay at one mine for long. It always looked to him like the grass was greener elsewhere, and that is what sealed his doom.

When John and Jessie came to Grant Town, West Virginia, they moved into one of the mine company houses. It was a monstrous, creaky old place that the company hadn't been able to get anyone else to live in. The last miner who had occupied it years ago died in an accident in the mines and there was talk that the house was haunted. John just laughed at that. He told Jessie they needed all that space for the family they were going to have and he would fix the roof, the sagging front porch, and the rotten floor boards, and the house would be good as new. But Jessie, try as she would, never could seem to make the house look cheerful.

One winter morning Jackson took the lunch his wife had fixed for him and set off for work as usual. It was so cold he could see his breath curl in the air like tobacco smoke. Under his feet the ground was crisp and his boots slid now and then on puddles turned to dirty glass. He had some odd feelings on his way to the mine that morning and he mentioned them to his buddy, Tony Dominec. Although he had just left Jessie, it was like he missed her already. He couldn't understand why he felt so sad.

"You'd think you two was courtin'," joked Tony but he couldn't get a smile out of Jackson, who just shook his head and didn't say a word. They rode the buggy (a small locomotive used to haul coal cars), and when Dominec got off at his level he said, "Meetcha after work." Jackson, who was working one level down, nodded.

It was early afternon when Dominec heard a terrible explosion in the depths of the mine. It seemed to come from beneath his feet and the men near him began running. He ran with them as fast as he could through the tunnel toward the main line. There he saw other miners racing through the main tunnel. Had a fire started on the level below? Would it spread? Would the main tunnel soon be filled with smoke?

Just ahead of him he saw men jumping into the buggy. His chest hurt, his legs felt as if they would give way under him, but he kept running and he managed to get into one of the last cars. When he reached the surface, he began looking for Jackson but he was nowhere to be found. By now wisps of smoke were coming out of the mouth of the mine.

The next morning there were knots of people standing around the entrance to the tunnel—the families of miners who had not come out on the buggy and several of the top men in the coal company. Jessie Jackson was there with her two little boys, waiting to hear whether the rescue crew that had gone into the mine would find any of the missing men still alive. Finally, they came out of the mine. They had found the place were the explosion had occurred, but the men near it had all been burned to death and John Jackson was one of them.

Times were hard and Jessie had only a little money to support herself and the two children. The spring after John's death she married Bill James, who had been one of her husband's close friends. Jessie would get up early, pack Bill's lunch, and off he would go to work at the mines. Then she would go back to bed for a while. About six months after her remarriage, Jessie began to see the ghost of her first husband. Each morning after she went back to bed the ghost would appear in a rocking chair near her. He would sit there staring for a while and then disappear. Jessie was so frightened she couldn't move. This went on for over a month, until she became more and more upset and had to be treated by the mining company doctor.

The doctor thought a change might be good for her and advised her to leave Grant Town for a few weeks and go home to visit her parents. When she returned, she and her husband moved into a new house about half a mile from her old home. Several weeks went by and much to her relief the ghost did not appear. But one morning she had just gone back to bed when she happened to look over at the rocker and there sat the apparition of her dead husband. She screamed and the specter disap-

peared, but the very next morning it was there again.

"What do you want? Tell me!" the terrified Mrs. James cried out.

The ghost motioned with his hand for her to come with him. Upset as she was, she put on her coat quickly and began to follow the shadowy figure down the road. The ghost kept ten or fifteen feet ahead of her, drifting noiselessly but purposefully along, there was no mistaking the fact that the spirit of her first husband seemed to know where it was going. Despite her fear she went on, and when the ghost turned off on the road that led to the mine, she turned, too.

As she arrived, she was just in time to see her second husband standing with a group of other miners waiting to get into the buggy that would take them into the mine. She called him over to her and explained how she had been led here by the ghost. Her husband became angry, for by now he thought all of this was some sort of foolishness. But Jessie began to tremble so, that he decided to take her to the doctor himself.

About lunchtime, when Bill and Jessie returned to the mine, they saw a crowd gathered around the entrance. Some of the women were crying as they held babies in their arms while others had children clinging to their skirts. Right after they had left, ten men had been buried in slate that had fallen from the roof of one of the tunnels, the very tunnel Bill James would have been working in that day. Jessie fell into her husband's arms and began to sob with relief.

If it had not been for the ghost of her first husband, her second would have died along with the other miners. They were both convinced that his ghost had returned from the dead to save Bill James's life, and from then on they placed flowers on his grave regularly.

The Ghosts of Shut-In Creek

Black Mountain, North Carolina

There is a place near Hot Springs in Madison County, North Carolina, that's haunted, "been haunted since I was a boy," said the white-haired old man.

"It may have started right after what happened to my uncle. He worked in a manganese mine up beyond Hot Springs at what they called Dry Branch. One mornin' they let my uncle down in the mine with the wooden box. He'd go down to the bottom, dig out manganese, and load it in the box until it was full and then they'd windlass the box back up.

"When a man would fill the box full, he'd shake the rope, and they kept waitin' and waitin' for my uncle to shake that rope but he never did. They began to holler down into the shaft and it was like a voice would holler up, but it was just their own calls comin' back at them. My uncle never did answer.

"Finally, they put hooks on ropes and let themselves down, and after awhile they managed to bring him up. But he was dead. Nobody knew for sure, but some said gas must have formed down there the night before and that's what killed him.

Shut-In Creek.

"They brought him up to the little old log house on the side of the mountain where he lived and they laid him out, a corpse. There was a real crowd there that night. Some sat inside with the body. Others just stood around the outside the house. I took a turn sittin' inside. Always heard you ought to do that to keep the cats off the corpse, but the lamp in that room kept goin' out even after my aunt brought in a fresh cleaned one. That light goin' out began to work on me some, so I asked her to get someone else to take my chair and set a spell and I went on outdoors.

"We were all standin' around talkin' when someone called out, 'Looky there, comin' right down the mountain!' I looked and saw this big light. Then it started to roll over and over and it was big as a barrel. It was just a-rollin' comin' down toward us. It rolled over and over and over and everybody began to holler. But not my uncle's brother, Ben, and it was comin' at him p'int-blank.

"I don't know whether he'd been drinkin' or what, but he begun to curse that light with it rollin' off the hill toward him. And when he did, well, it hit him, knocked him down, and just kept on rollin' right down the side of the mountain and across the road. Some of them boys standin' nearby lit out runnin' and those of us that stayed 'cause we were too scared to move, we picked Ben up and took him inside. But he never did recover and he died later that night.

"The home place is still there near Shut-In Creek, and it's been haunted ever since. Comin' along that road through there at night certain times of the year, certain nights, you could hear people talkin'. I was comin' through there one night—my, it was dark—and I heard some people talkin' and it sounded like there was a passel of them. It was right near my uncle's house. I kept walkin' expectin' to meet somebody, but I never did meet anybody. I told some folks about that later and a lot of people said, 'Why, I've heard that talkin' many a time.'

"You go about four miles beyond Hot Springs and then you turn to the left. That's Shut-In Creek and the haunted place is down aways about five miles. I wouldn't walk through there again at night, no matter what you gave me. They say the talkin' still goes on near that farm. You hear voices that seem like they move along the road right near you, but you never see a livin' soul."

Highway 19, Where Apparitions Still Ride

Flatwoods, West Virginia

The driver of the truck tried his CB radio again. "Breaker 19, Breaker 19, for north-bounder on Highway 19." Another West Virginia trucker's voice crackled back over the CB radio. "You got a south-bounder. This is the Big Driver." "How's it lookin' over your shoulder, good buddy?" asked Craig Tolliver. "It's clean and green back to Roanoke" came the reply. This was trucker's CB lingo for the fact that there were no patrol cars, accidents, or hazards over the stretch of road Tolliver would soon be traveling.

He had heard some weird stories about this area. His truck tended to hug the inside curve of the mountain road for he knew that a steep drop lay to the left of his cab. A few miles ahead was the hill that had brought death to more than one driver—two of them truckers like himself. It was not the road itself that presented the hazard. It was something far more mystifying.

His big trailer truck began the slow climb up the hill. Why should he be so apprehensive? He had driven this road near Flatwoods, West Virginia, many a time and the trip had always been uneventful. Surely it was only chance that there had been more than one accident along here. The truck went more slowly than usual tonight. Did it too feel reluctant to reach the stretch of highway ahead? What foolishness, he thought. He was overtired, for there was always tension in driving a truck this heavily loaded, and the steel girders he was carrying weighed over twenty-two tons. No wonder the truck was slow to respond on the up grade and tended to hurtle forward as he went down the hills.

Tolliver strained to see ahead. Now he was approaching the crest of the hill. As he reached it, he saw a sight so amazing he could hardly believe his eyes. Halfway down the incline, in his lane, was a wagon pulled by four horses. On the seat was a man and beside him a woman with long hair wearing a white dress. He realized with horror that there was not a way in the world he could avoid hitting that wagon.

He was in low gear, and although he knew it was futile, he pressed the brake as hard as he could. As he went down the grade coming closer and closer to the wagon, his brakes began to burn. Why didn't the wagon turn into the other lane? It contin-

ued its slow and measured pace. He thought of trying to go around it but he knew the weight of the steel girders would send him hurtling over the embankment. He would never be able to pull back in his own lane ahead of it.

He knew in another half minute the couple and their horses would all be one indistinguishable, bloody mass beneath the huge wheels of his truck. Tolliver felt a sudden wave of nausea and as if he were about to black out. In another second he would feel the impact. There was no way to avoid the collision.

Then, much to his astonishment, horses, wagon, and the couple all disappeared at the very moment he was braced for the impact! The moon came out and the road was illuminated behind him. As he looked in his mirror he could see that there was nothing there. What had happened? Where had the wagon and the couple gone? He knew that he had seen them as clearly as he had ever seen anything in his entire life.

It was only a short distance down the road to the truck stop where he had sometimes paused to refuel or for a cup of hot coffee. He needed that coffee tonight as he had never needed it before. When he lifted it steaming hot to his lips, his hands shook so that they spilled the coffee on the counter.

"You seem pretty shaken up, fellow, what's the trouble?" said a voice next to him. He turned to look at the man who had spoken.

"You a trucker?" he asked him. The man said, "No, I'm from over at Flatwoods, a few miles from here. Just thought I'd stop in and grab a sandwich."

Tolliver shook his head as if he would clear his mind.

"You know, if I didn't have good sense, I'd say I been seeing things and ought to be put away."

"What do you mean?"

Had it been another trucker he would have been too embarrassed to talk about it, but what difference did this old man make? He'd go back to the boondocks of Flatwoods, West Virginia, and nobody in his company would ever be any the wiser.

"You won't believe this, but comin' down that road a few miles back I was dead sure I was goin' to run right over the top of a wagon pulled by four horses." The man didn't look surprised.

"Was there a couple on the seat and the girl wearing a white dress?"

"There sure was," said the suprised Tolliver. "How'd you know that?"

"I've heard that story ever since I was a child. I was on that road one night when I was a young man on my way home from calling on my girl. It was bright moonlight and up ahead of me I saw an old wagon moving slowly up the hill. There was a man and a girl in a white dress with long yellow hair hanging to her waist. Their wagon was pulled by four white horses and it was loaded down with heaps of things like pioneers would carry. Those horses were milk white and when they came closer I could see they wore black harnesses with shiny brass studs. It was the strangest sight I ever saw. Just about the time I was close enough to hail them, that wagon disappeared and there was nothing on the road at all. It was a sight I'll never forget if I live to

Truck drivers never know when the phantom will be around the next curve on Highway 19.

be a hundred. Every now and then somebody sees it. My grandfather told me when that road was no more than a trail, a young couple decided to settle up in here and they were on their way to camp for the night near Hacker's Creek when a band of Indians attacked and killed them, leaving their bodies beside the road.

"Every so often, when the moon is bright on certain nights, I've heard tell of that wagon being seen on top of the hill and it has caused some bad accidents there. Sometimes, I wonder about that couple, who they were and why they keep coming back."

The old man shook his head, drained the last drop from his coffee mug, and left.

The Mysterious Face on the Wall

Grant Town, West Virginia

Nick Yelchick would have laughed if you had told him he would ever see a ghost. He was a big, strapping fellow who liked to brag a lot, and if he had too much to drink, it was better to stay away from him. After five years of working for the railroad, in March of 1927 he lost his job and began to find that the bottle helped him forget it. He would stop at a bootleggers in the late afternoon, have a few drinks, and then head home with his own jug.

Whenever he was drunk he would get angry over trifles, beat his wife, and tear up the house. This went on for several months. In the daytime he went out looking for work and finally was able to get one of the West Virginia mines to take him on.

132

The first week everything seemed to go well. The hours were long and the work took plenty of physical strength, but that didn't bother him. He had always made friends quickly, and although the other men would wink at each other when Nick started bragging, most of them liked him. And, at home things were better because he wasn't drinking.

But on Friday at lunch he asked one of his buddies to punch his timecard for him after work that afternoon for he wanted to get to his liquor supplier. His friend promised to do so.

Nick sat down to eat his lunch, and as he was eating one of the sandwiches Anna had packed for him, he began to think of some of the other tunnels where the men had been working that might be easier to mine.

He went down to the level below his own tunnel and inspected the walls as he walked. Other tunnels led off the main one and he turned down one of these, then down another and another before he realized he had lost his way. Aware he was lost, he began to panic and try desperately to get back to the main line. He had walked for several hours when the thought struck him that nobody would be looking for him because he had asked his buddy, John Avangio, to punch his timecard for him. No one would know he was still down in the mine.

After he had walked until what must have been late that night, his light burned out. Now he was in total darkness and he lost his self-control, shouting and shouting until his voice became a whisper. He knew he should wait until morning but he couldn't

stop. Finally, he was so exhausted he was too tired to walk any further. He slumped down against the wall of the tunnel and fell fast asleep.

He was awakened by a strange dream. He had dreamed that he saw his wife's face before him and as he stared into the blackness he saw a luminous spot gradually take shape on the wall of the tunnel and his wife's face stared back at him. He put his arms across his face, convinced that he must still be dreaming, and then he heard her voice and she was saying, "Follow me." Her face began to move along the wall of the tunnel and, frightened though he was, he managed to get up and walk toward it. The eyes shone out at him and the lips seemed to move again forming the words, "Follow me, follow me."

Down one tunnel and then another he went, the face staying just ahead of him. This went on for what must have been over an hour until, at last, he found himself on the main line once more. He looked for the face but it had disappeared. When he arrived at the surface of the mine the night watchman said, "What you been doin' down there, Nick? Your wife was here lookin' for you yesterday, but I seen your card was punched and I told her you had left."

When Nick got home, the first thing he saw was his wife lying across the bed. He went over to wake her, thinking she must have been up all night. When he shook her she didn't move, and then he realized she was dead. On the kitchen table he found a note that said, "Nick, I thought you would stop drinking when you got this job but now I know better."

Nick Yelchick collapsed in a chair, and with his arms on the table he began sobbing, for he knew now that it was his wife's ghost that had come to lead him out of the mine and save his life. From that day on he was a changed man, until he died in Grant Town over twenty years later.

The Specter's Vengeance

Ducktown, Tennessee

A few hours before John Lyons had loaded up the last of his ore at the Copperhill Mine at Ducktown, Tennessee. His blond hair fell over his eyes as he hunched forward, feeling the pull of his team of horses, for the load was a heavy one. He was a good-natured young man and the money he was making hauling ore would soon be enough for a small farm for himself and the girl in Kingsport whom he planned to marry. His mind dwelt happily upon these things.

But the ride to the river was not to be the quiet one he had expected and his musings were soon interrupted by apprehension.

Robbers had been waylaying wagons near here and driving the horses and wagons over the cliff after robbing the bodies of the dead drivers. Lyons, like most of the teamsters in eastern Tennessee and North Carolina, was well paid for hauling ore from the mine to the river dock. He patted his money belt uneasily, and as darkness fell across mountains and valleys, every shadow seemed ready to leap out at him.

Thinking he heard sounds other than the creaking of his wagon wheels, he looked around expecting to see robbers at any moment. It was not his imagination, for another wagon was following his. Acting on impulse he decided to pull over into the woods and let it pass. As he waited, he saw it come into view in the moonlight. It was loaded high with copper ore and on the seat sat the figure of a huge man. The fellow wore a dust-covered jacket, secured by one button, and a broad-brimmed, black felt hat.

Lyons stared curiously at the face, and at first glance was appalled by its pallor and staring eyes. But as he watched, the features seemed to spring to life. The mouth broke into a smile and the hollow eyes lit up. The features were strangely familiar. The man obviously meant him no harm and it was good to have company on this road, he thought gratefully.

But not far away from the landing on the river, where the boats were loaded to carry ore to the smelter in Chattanooga, the band of outlaws was already lying in wait. They stood well back in the brush along the banks of the creek where the road

from the mine crossed it. Whispering and grumbling they waited.

"I told you John Lyons would be the last teamster away from Ducktown tonight. Poor fellow, hauling that last lonesome load of copper to the landing," their leader smirked. But his words froze on his lips as he watched the wagon cross the ford. Neither the horse's hoofs nor the wagon wheels splashed the placid surface, but, instead, the wagon appeared to glide over the water.

"Must be turrible low water over that rock," one of the men said. Another spoke up. "Look at that driver, boys. Recognize him, Lem?"

"I think so, but I can't say for sure. He looks strung out, don't he?"

While they watched, a second wagon appeared and took the ford almost in one leap without a call to the horses or a splash. Just as the leader of the robber band raised his pistol, a third wagon appeared. The robbers by now were thoroughly bewildered, for they had expected only John Lyons. Almost as much in fear as to signal the attack, the leader pulled the trigger.

His men swept down, encircling the doomed wagons. In the manner Indians attack, they galloped in a circle around them. Almost in slow motion the three teamsters reached into their wagons and pulled out their rifles, each aiming in a different direction. Before they could fire, the encircling band of outlaws cut loose with their six-shooter revolvers.

The report of gunfire echoed off the mountainside and three of the robbers lay dead from

their own bullets. A moment later the wagons vanished as if they had never been there and the night was quiet. The silence was suddenly broken by the sound of a teamster whip and yet another wagon

rolled along, heading for the ford. The driver drove it with a certain bold abandon and a broad smile upon his face as he headed straight for the landing.

The remaining two outlaws were stunned. Surely, this must be Lyons' wagon and now things would go their way. They began emptying their revolvers at the driver who cracked his whip repeatedly in some sort of wild exultation.

He smiled gleefully as bullets whizzed toward him and his crackling whip gave off tiny sparks in the moonlight. "Keep on firing, boys!" he shouted. His whip touched the tree branches and sent them shivering and rustling. As John Lyons watched from a safe distance back beside the road, he thought he saw the tip of the whip stroke each· branch and the leaves sparkle like Fourth of July fireworks. Red and gold bursts of flame, followed by tiny sparks, floated down, struck the rocks in the stream, and faded into extinction. Then all was quiet, for the last of the robbers had fled.

John Lyons was filled with awe. He had recognized some of the drivers of the wagons that passed him, but the reason for his astonishment was that they were all dead! They were the drivers who had been murdered here during the past two years. If it had not been for them, by now he too would probably have been murdered. His life had been saved by a phantom wagon train.

The Angel of Death

Mountains, South Carolina

Patty McCoy was chilled to the bone, but it was not the September night as much as the words she had just heard: "Beware of the cemetery gates, for they will bring death!" She was terrified, for the gates of the cemetery were opposite the McCoy house. The only light in the room came from the kerosene lamp. The witchwoman's skin was seamed and leathery. One eye stared fiercely straight ahead and the other veered off into space with a fiercely malevolent look.

"I see you as a child full of joy," said the woman, "Then as a young girl, when you first met your husband. You wore a blue crocheted shawl the night he asked you to marry him. Isn't that so?" Patty nodded. "He's still a likely-favored man. Is he not?" Patty's eyes filled with tears at the thought of him sitting at sundown on the porch, his banjo in his lap, playing the tunes he loved. He had been ill for almost a year and that was the reason she had come here for advice. Today Bradley was to go to the hospital.

"There is one thing you must never let happen," warned the old woman in her rasping voice, head thrust forward. "I know your homeplace well and the gates of that cemetery are right across the road from it. When they take him to the hospital, don't you let them open that gate. If you do, he's going to die. For what's inside those gates will never rest until it gets him."

Patty put her hand over her mouth to keep from screaming. People had always said, "That Patty, She ain't afeard of nothin'." But now she was afraid. She put a fifty-cent piece in the woman's hand and left.

All she could think about was whether they had come yet to get Bradley. She had been gone for almost two hours. The witchwoman had prepared bits of bone, feathers, roots before she would tell her what to do about Bradley. Patty had no sooner reached the edge of the woods and the open field across which she could see the house when she gave a shriek. For out in front of the porch was a small, dusty ambulance to take him to Louisville. She began to run. Her breath came fast and her heart pounded. She was halfway up the road to the house when the front door opened and two men bearing a stretcher with Bradley carried it down the front steps and placed it in the back of the ambulance.

She screamed out at them, "Wait! Don't take my Bradley 'til I tell ye about the gate." The men looked at her strangely but waited. Now she stood beside them and for a moment was too breathless to warn them about what the witchwoman had told her. She looked at Bradley lying so still on the stretcher, his face the color of putty.

"Kin ye holp him?" asked Patty. The ambulance driver, a tall, red-haired man with watery blue eyes, looked down at her expressionlessly and nodded.

"Well, there ain't no turn-around up here," said Patty. "And when ye git that ambulance down to the road, whatever ye do, don't open the gate of the cemetery to back in. Do ye hear me?"

The driver and his helper got in the ambulance and Patty watched as they backed it down the narrow mountain trail. When they reached the road they must have tried three or four times to back and cut sharp so the ambulance could head out. One of the men finally stood by the side of the road hollering at the other, "If'n you'll just open that gate, we won't have no trouble." But Patty had taken down the shotgun from over the fireplace just as a precaution, run down the road after them, and now stood squarely in front of the gate.

The driver of the ambulance looked at her and at the shotgun, cut the wheels of the ambulance hard, and this time he made it. Patty stood with her back against the cemetery gate and watched the ambulance until it was out of sight. Then she turned and gazed down the road and up the hill toward the cemetery. It was dusk, and as she looked up toward the markers on the crest, she shuddered. What could possibly be up there that could harm

her Bradley? A wind sprang up rustling the tree leaves. It felt chilly for this time of year. Patty shivered and watched the shadows from the cypress trees begin to merge into the coming darkness. Then she turned and walked up the road toward home.

A week later she went to town with Joe Hartley and they brought Bradley back from the hospital in his old pick-up truck. Bradley looked lots better and talked like he felt pretty good, but by the time he was jounced all the way home in the truck, Patty saw he was tired. He wouldn't lie down none though. Said he had to get out and hoe their fall garden. She saw he just needed to do something, so she let him be.

Bradley acted like he was tired a lot of the time and he was a little "tetchy" which wasn't like him. Before he always let her know he was sorry if he saw something he'd said discomfited her, but he didn't talk much now and seldom said anything about the future, like how he was going to buy the land next to theirs and clear it or build another room on to the small cabin nor did he ever hug her about the waist as he used to do and tell her she was still the "likeliest favored gal" he ever saw.

Less than two month later he was down in the bed again, so tired that the littlest thing seemed to make him too weak to lift his head. The doctor wanted him to go to the hospital and Patty wanted to try to get him on the mend at home, but finally she agreed that he should go. She waited with Bradley, holding his hand until the ambulance could get there. It was a large, new ambulance this time, but the tall, white-faced, red-haired man got out with a little, short, chesty fellow who looked well able to handle a stretcher even with a big man on it. Patty pushed back a strand of hair that lay across her husband's forehead and then with a jerky, self-conscious motion bent down and kissed his cheek. The men put the stretcher in the back of the ambulance. Patty felt like she was going to cry, and, turning, she went into the house. She heard the slam of the two doors as the men got in the front and the quiet purr of the motor as the ambulance started backing down the road.

Then, she flung herself across the patchwork quilt on the old walnut bed, but she couldn't cry. Her chest hurt and began to heave. She lay there holding her arms tightly around her and shook, but no tears came.

Suddenly, she recalled the gate and what the witchwoman had told her. She was out the door in an instant and running down the rutted trail that led from the house to the road, when she saw the short, heavy set man jump out of the ambulance and start for the gate. She screamed with all her might, but the wind only blew the words back at her. The gate swung open, the ambulance backed in, and was out and gone. The autumn sunlight struck its massive chrome front and nearly blinded her.

She ran toward the gate, pulled it closed, and then leaned on it, looking toward the hill where the bodies of relatives, friends, and parents were buried, She had not been able to keep the gate closed even after what the witchwoman had told her. Patty leaned against it, feeling as if she was going to faint.

Now the wind sprang up with a vengeance. The leaves that had been green and tender two months before when she had stood at this gate made the harsh, rustling sounds of sandpaper rubbing together, like the eerie rasp of the witchwoman's voice saying over and over, "Don't let them open the cemetery gate! Don't let them open the cemetery gate! Don't let them open it!" The voice within her grew more and more shrill until

she felt that she was floating on a sea of madness. Bradley, Bradley . . . she knew she had failed him.

On top of the hill stood a small knot of people huddled together to escape the biting wind of the winter day. It was the graveyard prayer for Bradley McCoy who had died in the ambulance on the way to the hospital. Patty stood near the grave, head bowed.

She was convinced that something had come out of this cemetery three days before. Some dark, stalking thing that refused to be thwarted and it had claimed Bradley McCoy.